THE PATH TO THE NEW

HERMOPOLIS

The Path to the New Hermopolis:
The History, Philosophy, and Future of the City of Hermes

First published in 2019 by

RUBEDO PRESS
AUCKLAND
NEW ZEALAND
WWW.RUBEDO.PRESS

Minor revisions, August 2020.

ISBN: 978-0-9951245-0-9 (softcover)

Design and Typography by Aaron Cheak

The front cover image is taken from a relief on the ceiling of the Temple of Hathor at Dendera, Egypt. The eight figures on the left depict the four gods and four goddesses of the Ogdoad: the primordial creative forces of the Hermopolitan cosmogony which gave their name to the city *Khmnw* (Khemenu), known to the Greeks as Hermopolis.

SCRIBE SANGUINE QUIA SANGUIS SPIRITUS

THE PATH TO THE NEW

HERMOPOLIS

THE HISTORY, PHILOSOPHY, AND FUTURE
OF THE CITY OF HERMES

Mervat Nasser

MD, MPHIL, FRCPSYCH

RUBEDO
Auckland 2019

Contents

*I made an enclosure around the park
lest it be trampled by the rabble
for it is the birthplace
of every god*

—PETOSIRIS—

PREFACE

WHEN I WAS BORN, MY FATHER NAMED ME MERVAT, a Turkish corruption of the word *Marw* (or *Marwa*), the holy well from which Abraham's wife managed to fetch water for her son (Ismael in the *Koran*, and Isaac in the *Old Testament*). Only later would I find out that *Marw* is in fact a special type of stone that points to the presence of water either underneath it or in its vicinity. This is the same meaning as the term Herm or Herma, the origin of the name Hermes.

As a child, my attention was drawn to a commercial on Egyptian television in the form of a short, animated film set to beautiful music and lyrics. It was modelled on a simple fairy tale of a young prince who fell in love with a beautiful young princess, and the only way for him to win her heart was to obtain a small treasure hidden in a cave in a remote part of the land, the road to which was lined with all sorts of risks.

The treasure was in fact nothing but a bottle of perfume called Kismet, a word which means 'destiny' in Arabic. At that time, I did not know anything about the *Book of Thoth*, the ancient book of learning which the Egyptians attributed to Thoth, the god of wisdom who brought the arts of civilisation to humankind. According to legend, the *Book of Thoth* was Egypt's treasure; it was lost and never recovered.

I did not envisage too, that one day I would become a psychiatrist—one of those who claim to have some understanding of the human soul (*psychē* in Greek). In Greek mythology, Psyche was driven by curiosity to know the nature of her lover, Eros, and in her pursuit of such knowledge, *light* was necessary to see through the *darkness* of the night that envelops it. This is the journey of the soul in her quest to gain the sum of knowledge that is hidden inside, the inner vision or *insight* that guides us all out of darkness to the safe shores of wisdom.

The same journey took me to that part of Egypt where my father is buried, and wisdom was born. It took me to Hermopolis, the place where *being* is seen as perpetual *becoming*, and the knowledge of yesterday is nothing but a well of inspiration for tomorrow.

DR. MERVAT NASSER
NEW HERMOPOLIS, EGYPT

THE PATH TO THE NEW
HERMOPOLIS

Among the Egyptians, the first month of the year is named after him (and) a city was founded by him that is now called Hermopolis in Greek. He is called Trismegistus because he was the greatest philosopher.

CORPUS HERMETICUM

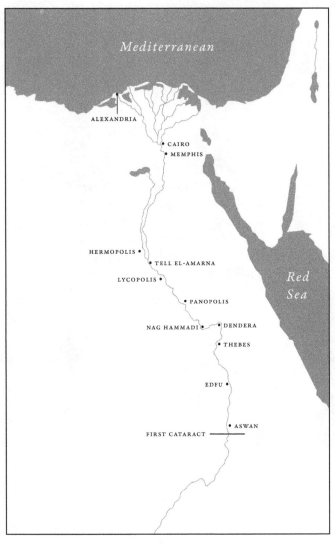

Mediterranean

ALEXANDRIA

CAIRO
MEMPHIS

Red
Sea

HERMOPOLIS
TELL EL-AMARNA
LYCOPOLIS

PANOPOLIS

NAG HAMMADI
DENDERA
THEBES

EDFU

ASWAN
FIRST CATARACT

EGYPT

I

HERMES

and Hermopolis

From Thoth to Hermes

FOR THE EGYPTIANS, the word, or *logos*, was synonymous with the essence of life and the seed of all things. Thoth or Tehuti was the 'lord of the divine words' who invented the hieroglyphs and who also put thought and speech into form, encapsulating the 'in-formation' of the world into words. He is considered the author of the legendary *Book of Thoth* (Jasnow & Zauzich 2005), which contained all the Egyptian mysteries and presumed to be the predecessor of the famous *Hermetica*.

> The word fell on fertile waters
> making them pregnant with all forms.
> HERMETICA

It was no coincidence that the Egyptian alphabet took the shape of birds that were seen as capable of flying high into the sky to mediate between the knowledge of heaven and earth, between god and humanity.

This form of 'picture writing' made it possible for the Egyptians to denote ideas in linguistic signs, and to render their writing primarily as a symbolic means of communication. It was also a kind of cryptic code that was meant to ensure both the secrecy and the sacredness of what is written, for it demanded the effort of learning to prove one's worthiness of the wisdom it contained.

> Write the wisdom you have understood
> In hieroglyphic characters,
> carved on stone in the holy sanctuary.
> HERMETICA

Thoth was identified with the moon, the place where our memory resides. The moon tells the story of humanity, beginning with birth and ending with death, through the process of growth and becoming:

> Hail to you, moon, Thoth
> Who relates what was forgotten
> And remembers the fleeting moment
> Whose words endure forever.
> HORAMHEB'S HYMN TO THOTH

FIGURE 1.

*Ibis-headed form of Thoth,
'Lord of divine words'; inventor of
hieroglyphs, writing, & the sciences;
god of the moon, wisdom, & magic.*

Thoth was therefore the measurer of time and the counter of days. Through the phases of the moon, time was measured as a moving aspect of eternity in its ever-recurring cycle.

It is interesting that the name of the year for the Egyptians is *renpet*, which literally means 'that which rejuvenates itself', as it signals the beginning of time and the return once more to creation. This means that every time we begin anew, we are in fact trying to remind ourselves of this *mythical first time* that was our beautiful beginning, or in other words, our true self (Hornung 1992; Cashford 2003).

Thoth was also the reflection of the sun (Ra), in whose absence he fills the darkness of the night with his moonlight. He was the great astronomer and record keeper who marked the cycles of perceived time as mirrored by the movements of celestial bodies:

> The sun said it would shine all day,
> providing laughter as a source of joy
> for both mortal minds
> and the boundless universe itself
> The moon promised sleep and silence
> And to shine at night.
> Saturn offered justice and necessity.
> Jupiter gave peace and Mars struggle.
> Venus proffered love and pleasure.
> HERMETICA

However, when it came to inventing the calendar, Thoth did not choose the lunar cycle; instead he chose a solar calendar. The first Egyptian calendar was one of 365 days, and begansh with a month named after Thoth (Bomhard 1999).

This calendar has remained in current use till our present time. It is the basis of the Egyptian Coptic calendar, which begins with the month Thot/Tut, as well as the Egyptian farming calendar that is used by nearly all Egyptian farmers today.

The symbols of Thoth include the baboon, which might have been based on the Egyptians' observation that this particular animal tends to produce a special sound at sunrise, as if greeting the light of the sun. The baboon's noted intelligence and its proximity to humans could have been another reason.

In *Egypt's Legacy* (1997), Michael Rice discusses the Egyptians' attitude to animals from a Jungian perspective, which according to him revealed much about their (as well as our) collective psyche. Here, the 'big ape' was the ultimate archetype of the 'wise old man'. According to Jung, this wisdom was neither a question of belief nor of knowledge, but the 'agreement of our thinking with the primordial images of our unconscious' (Jung 1944).

Thoth is also often depicted in temples, tomb engravings, and papyri as a human being with an ibis' head. The choice of the symbolic ibis bird invited several explanations. One of them was attributed to the shape of the ibis' beak, which resembled the crescent moon, thus representing Thoth in his lunar form.

The ibis was also metaphorically regarded as the scribe's finger, suggesting that the bird was the actual writer of Thoth's thoughts as portrayed in ancient Egyptian literature:

FIGURE 2.
Baboon-formed image of Thoth.

The finger of the scribe is the ibis beak,
beware of brushing it aside.

THE TEACHING OF AMENOPHIS

Cashford (2015) commented on the fact that most gods
of inspiration were given a bird form, either with the heads
or wings of birds, an image thought to fit their role as *magical
messengers* connecting what is above with that which is below,
namely the sublime with the mundane.

Another suggestion was the connection between the ibis
and the human heart, for it was noted that the Egyptians,
in some instances, used to draw an ibis instead of the heart,
which was also used occasionally as synonymous with Thoth
himself, who was described in a text in the temple of Karnak
as the 'one who knows what lives in the heart' (Boylan 1922).

The association of Thoth with the human heart brings us
to his role in the judgment of the dead, particularly the act of
the weighing of the heart, in which the heart of the deceased
is weighed in the scales against the feather of Maat, the symbol of balance and truth. If the weight of the heart was found
to be equal to that of the feather, the deceased is deemed by
Thoth as having led a 'true life', namely having been true of
heart and tongue. This is the time, when the integrity of the
deceased is vindicated, and Thoth 'opens the ways' for the soul
of the deceased to join eternity (Boylan 1922).

It is important however not to forget that the Egyptian's
image for the soul is also a bird—the *Ba*-bird—which is normally depicted in the scenes of the judgment of the dead as
hovering over the deceased as if carrying with it the promise of

a union between the temporary individual soul and the eternal world soul (Cashford 2015).

The issue of personal integrity and the concept of integration as the *making whole of what has been divided or torn apart*, clearly takes us to yet another role of Thoth, namely the healer and the insight giver. According to the Egyptian myth of Isis and Osiris, Horus sought to avenge the murder of his father Osiris, who was dismembered by Set. In the conflict between Horus and Set, Horus was reported to have lost his eye. This loss necessitated the intervention of Thoth, who successfully *restored* Horus' Eye:

> I am Thoth who brings justice,
> who healed the Sacred Eye.
> COFFIN TEXTS

The loss of the eye in this mythical fight was meant to convey to us the limitations of our seeing through an outer eye, when revenge for the victim is normally justified and considered to be the only answer. The 'loss of the eye' here is symbolic of the loss of this outer, limited eye in order to gain instead an inner eye—a better-seeing eye that allows for re-vision of one's position and the ultimate realisation of the futility of revenge (Nasser 2004).

The struggle between Horus and Set in this myth eventually ends with their reconciliation (Jackson 2011). And this balancing, reconciliatory act would not have been possible without the intervention of Thoth—who has been described in the beautiful *Hymn to Thoth* that is engraved on the statue of Horemheb at the Metropolitan Museum of Art (New York) as the one who 'changes turmoil into peace' (Lichtheim 1976).

The eye of Horus is now a familiar Egyptian symbol, associated with both healing and insight, but above all with the integration of opposites. It is no surprise therefore to find that the Egyptian name for the eye of Horus is *Udjat*, which is literally translated as 'integrity' (Nasser 2004).

In Hellenistic Egypt, Thoth was equated with Hermes, and came to be seen in his familiar Greek travelling attire: the famous winged hat and sandals. In Roman times he was associated with the god Mercurius, the divinity of border crossing and alchemical transformations.

In Greek literature, Hermes, as in the case with Thoth, is also associated with the moon and has the gift of the word (*logos*). But above all he is the messenger of the gods and the god who guides departed souls through the underworld (Slavenburg 2012).

The questions that now arise are: when did Thoth become Hermes, and why was the assimilation between the two deemed necessary? And when did Hermes become 'thrice great'? The answer to these questions are clearly connected with the emergence of the Hellenistic age that required an integration between the Egyptian and Greek mentalities to develop a new world view that had the capacity to respond to the major cultural and political changes that took place around that time. It is important to note, however, that the description of Thoth as 'thrice great' appeared earlier, in the Egyptian *Book of Thoth* (Slavenburg 2012). The term 'twice great' was also given to Thoth in the relief depicting the myth of Horus at the Temple of Edfu (Blackman & Fairman 1946). And yet the epithet 'thrice-great' (Greek *trismegistos*), regardless of the various historical accounts, was only meant to convey the greatness of the god's wisdom and learning:

> Mercury, who is also called Hermes,
> Said: I will make humankind intelligent
> I will convey to them wisdom
> And knowledge of the truth,
> I will never cease to benefit humanity.
> HERMETICA

The City of Hermes

Contrary to the Greek notion of the city (*polis*) as an independent political and social entity, the ancient Egyptians saw their cities—and indeed their whole world—as cosmic. Egyptian cities were regarded as enlightening spaces, with temples known as 'houses of life' entrusted to a class of scribes who dedicated their lives to the pursuit of wisdom. This was the reason why, long before Hellenistic times, so many Greek philosophers flocked to Egypt to study among the temples and sages (Hansen 2006; Quirke 2011; Lachman 2011).

The continuous rivalry and the warfare between the various Greek city states threatened the survival of the independent Greek city. By the fifth and fourth centuries BCE, Ath-

FIGURE 3.

Hermes-Mercurius: Græco-Roman god of eloquence, travel, language, & exchange. From 'Architecture, peinture & sculpture de la Maison de Ville d'Amsterdam', 1719.

ens lost its power—initially to the Spartans and then to the Macedonians—and the notion of the city state was no longer viable. The world became much larger, less personal, and more complex. Identities were changed and challenged, calling for a shift in attitude and a change in world perception (Kreis 2000; Hansen 2006).

The situation became increasingly more difficult with the conquest of Egypt by Alexander the great in 332 BCE. The Greeks arrived in a country that was already beaming with different races, cultures, and ideologies. Egyptians, Persians, Greeks, Jews, and others lived together—or at least had to learn to live together—a situatution not dissimilar to our world today (Lachman 2011).

The small size of the city state or *polis* had to give way to the *cosmopolis*—the 'world city'—namely: a city with a worldview that could offer its citizens a kind of therapy or a way of life that was able to cope with the rising challenges (Kreis 2000; Nasser 2012). A merging of the Egyptian and the Greek mentalities had to take place, and this gave rise to a new, syncretistic consciousness: a Hellenistic mindset that believed in the possibility of a non-territorial, integrated new world. Although Alexandria became the cosmic city and the capital of this new age, the philosophy behind the development of Alexandria as a *cosmopolis* was rooted in a much older settlement in the south of Egypt. It was known to the Greeks as Hermopolis.

THE CONCEPTUAL INTANGIBLE CITY

The City of Hermes or Hermopolis is known today by its Arabic name, Ashmunin, which is derived from the Coptic *Shumnu*, which in turn comes from the ancient Egyptian *Khmnu*, meaning the 'city of eight' or Ogdoad.

Mythologically, the Ogdoad are made of four masculine deities and their feminine counterparts, who represent the primordial creative forces whose 'marriage' enabled harmony to be born. These four pairs of divinities are:

Nun and Nunet (fluidity and water)
Heh and Hehet (infinity and air)
Kek and Keket (darkness and fire)
Amen and Amenet (hiddenness and earth)

The identification of these forces with the elements that constitute nature (water, air, fire, earth) is simply a way to make abstract notions accessible to the mind via a mythical construct. However, the true focus of the Egyptian mind was more on the attributes of these elements: namely the infinite, invisible, hidden, and undifferentiated world, or in other words, the world that is 'yet to exist' (Hornung 1992).

And for the world to exist, it was necessary to integrate and harmonize all its opposing parts which can only be achieved through order, proportion, and balance—concepts that are all subsumed within the ancient Egyptian principle of Maat, the consort of Thoth who is responsible for the *harmonious* birth of the universe (Kaster 1993; Nasser 2004).

Harmony for the Egyptians was defined as the balanced, pleasing state that imparts both *joy* and *beauty*. This was very much in keeping with the expression of the ancient scribe's 'longing for Hermopolis', a place that is described as 'pleasant to live':

> O Thoth, take me to Ashmunin (Hermopolis),
> to the joyous city where it is pleasant to live...
> to the well for one who thirsts in the desert.
> HYMNS, PRAYER AND SONGS (Foster 1996).

FIGURE 4.
*The hare hieroglyph, which forms
the Egyptian word for 'being'* 𓃹 *(wn).*

In his book, *Freedom and Destiny* (2012), the existential psychoanalyst Rollo May defined joy as the 'opening of the soul to new possibilities'; in other words the 'unfolding of life to awe and wonderment'. Curiously, the region where Hermopolis lies was literally known in ancient times as the place where 'goodness and beauty enter one's being'.

The county of Hermopolis was known as the Nome of Wenet, which means the 'district of the hare'—the animal of intelligent movements who dances beneath the moon and brings tides of luck (Richardson & Walker-John 2010). More profoundly, however, is the fact that the hieroglyphic sign of the hare, which is used to signify the word *wn*, is commonly translated as the 'essence of life' or 'being'.

In Egyptian imagery we sometimes see the *wn* hieroglyph encircled by the ouroboros—the serpent that swallows its own tail, which became a familiar Hermetic symbol of cyclicity and eternal return. The space between *wn* (being) and the ouroboros constitutes the world's horizons or the sphere of non-being, where being always has the potential of continually recalling, restoring, and renewing itself (Hornung 1992).

We also find the god Osiris—the quintessential Egyptian symbol of eternal renewal—referred to as *wn-nefer*. *Nefer* means both 'good' and 'beautiful', and thus *wn-nefer* can be translated as the 'beautiful/good being', or 'the one who brings good into being'. This leads us to believe that Hermopolis for the ancient Egyptians represented not only a joyous place, but also a 'place of beautiful renewal'.

Apart from these metaphorical and connotative associations, what is perhaps most important is the fact that Hermopolis is generally considered to be the place where the *Hermetica* first originated. Its author, after all, is none other than the great Thoth-Hermes himself.

The *Hermetica* (which has already been cited in this chapter) is a collection of philosophical writings that revolve around the nature of god, humankind, and the cosmos. In these texts, god is seen as the supreme mind who created the cosmos and entrusted humankind to continue with his creative work of bringing order and beauty to the world (Freke & Gandy 1999).

The focus of the *Hermetica* is on the unity of being, the interconnectedness of everything in the world, and the importance of preserving the balance of the universe through embracing its opposites. For humanity, it also carries a promise of spiritual elevation and renewal through knowledge and creativity. We are told that the Hermetic manuscripts were recovered and collected in the city of Alexandria around the second-to-third century CE. They were eighteen in number and came to be known to us as the *Corpus Hermeticum*, or simply the *Hermetica*.

The manuscripts of the *Hermetica* were mostly written in Greek, which initially gave rise to the notion that they were of Greek origin (a view that continued to dominate academic circles up until very recently). However, the scales were tipped towards an Egyptian origin with the recent discovery and subsequent publication of the Egyptian *Book of Thoth* (dated to the first century BC), which was written in both Hieratic and Demotic, which are different stages in the development of the ancient Egyptian script (Jasnow & Zauzich 2005). This evidence adds to the discovery of the Nag Hammadi Library in Upper Egypt in 1945, with its famous fund of Coptic Hermetic manuscripts (Robinson 1988).

THE TANGIBLE ARCHÆOLOGICAL CITY

Hermopolis was in fact the capital of the 'Nome of the Hare', the fifteenth Nome of Upper Egypt that stood on the borders of Upper and Lower Egypt, and for many ages was an important administrative and learning centre. Even the village where the ruins of Ashmunin-Hermopolis stand today is still called El-Idara in Arabic, which literally means the 'administrative centre'.

Archæologically, the history of Hermopolis can be traced back to the Old Kingdom and even to the first dynasty. However, the structural remains that are still present date from the Middle Kingdom and the New Kingdom (Bagnall & Rathbone 2004).

The city had its ups and downs throughout Pharaonic history, but enjoyed its vogue in Hellenistic Egypt when it was taken as a prototype of the cosmic city where different cultures and races could meet and cohabit peacefully. This state of *cultural fusion* is beautifully depicted on the walls of the famous Petosiris tomb in Tuna El-Gebel, where the scenes show Egyptian, Greek, and even Persian influences.

O, every prophet, every priest, every scholar
Who enters here and see this tomb
I built this tomb in this necropolis
Beside the great souls who are there.
INSCRIPTION FROM PETOSIRIS' TOMB
(Lichtheim 1980)

Petosiris was the chief scribal priest of Hermopolis under the reign of Alexander the Great, and his tomb—which takes the form of a small temple with a columned façade—was also the burial site of former generations of Hermopolitan scribes that belong to his family. Alongside Petosiris, there are other important tombs, in addition to the great labyrinthine catacombs that once housed scrolls of written scripture accompanied by mummified ibises and baboons—the symbols of Thoth (Bagnall & Rathbone 2004). Some of these still remain in place.

Prior to the burial site at Tuna El-Gebel—which is also known as Hermopolis West—it was customary in the Old and Middle Kingdoms for the royal scribes of Hermopolis to be buried in the necropolis of Deir el-Bersha or Bani Hassan. Both major sites lie in the vicinity of ancient Hermopolis.

The city of Hermes continued to flourish under the Romans, but afterwards its structures witnessed significant changes and alterations. Due to an unfortunate development, its stones were dismantled to be used as building materials for other purposes.

Ancient documents suggest that both Hermopolis and the neighbouring Roman city Antinopolis (which is five kilometers west of Hermopolis) were both built on the Nile, however Antinopolis is the only city that is still on the Nile, and in ancient times it was an important harbour for Hermopolis. Antinopolis became a Roman city under the Emperor Hadrian, who built it in commemoration of the death of his friend Antinous, who drowned in the Nile while apparently on his way to Hermopolis. Antinopolis is now a notable Coptic site with significant Christian monuments.

A few descriptions of ancient Hermopolis have survived in the works of Arab scholars. Some of these descriptions are awe-inspiring, such as the one in the *Picatrix*, the eleventh-century book of magic known as the *Ghayat-al-Hakim* (The Goal of the Wise), which is heavily based on Hermeticism, alchemy, and astrology. In this text, the city is described as having fruitful trees and a lighthouse with a 'spherical cupola' that flooded the city with a different coloured light each day of the week. It also had 'four gates guarded with statues of priests holding scrolls of scientific works', and whoever wanted to learn a science 'went to its particular statue, stroked it with his hand and then stroked his breast, thus transferring the science to himself' (Daly 2005).

Reports from European travellers regarding the ruins of Hermopolis (Ashmunin) started to appear in the seventeenth century. The First archæological map with a detailed description of Hermopolis was found in the French *Description de l'Égypte* by Jonard, a member of Napoleon's expedition of 1798–1799, with a description of the hall of columns and the temple of Thoth (Neret 2002).

THE GEO-HERMETICA BELT

The temple of Thoth, which is also known as the 'temple of elevated spirits', was supposedly built according to sacred mathematical measurements and served as a model for the famous Temple of Solomon. Remains of this temple can still be seen

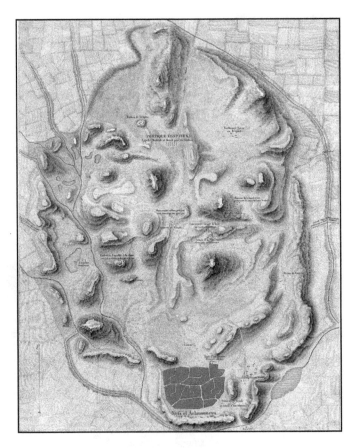

FIGURE 5.

*Topographical map of the ruins of Ashmunin
(Hermopolis Magna), Description de l'Egypte,
1809–1828.*

FIGURE 6.

Ruins of the temple at Hermopolis
Description de l'Egypte, 1809–1828.

in the present-day city of Ashmunin. It was re-dedicated to Amun and later to Alexander the Great under Ptolemaic rulership. Its remains stand with the ruins of a beautiful Roman Christian basilica (Bagnall & Rathbone 2004).

In the course of Egyptian history, the temple of Thoth was the subject of constant refurbishment and expansion. What remains of it today shows that the temple was rebuilt by Ramesses II (Nineteenth Dynasty, New Kingdom), using material provided by the neighbouring city of El-Amarna.

This is interesting inasmuch as Ramesses II was thought to be striving to bring Akhenaten's monotheistic doctrine back in line with the cosmic notion of the divine, in which the single god was hidden in the multiplicity of things, a sublime Hermetic notion that was clearly developed in the Ramesside period (Assmann 1997).

El-Amarna or Akhet-Aten (the Horizon of the Sun) was founded by Amenhotep IV (Eighteenth Dynasty, New Kingdom). Amenhotep changed his name to Akhen-Aten to make the word *aten* ('sun, light') integral to it. Despite what happened to the city due to abandonment and destruction, it is still considered to be the only ancient city in Egypt that has retained a good deal of its original internal plans. It was made up of temples, government establishments, palaces, homes, gardens, and burial tombs. A number of beautiful reliefs are still able to be seen here, the most famous of all depicting Akhenaten with his wife Nefertiti and his daughters, with their arms stretched out to the sun.

Akhenaten is always regarded as the most controversial figure in Egyptian history. Was he indeed the first prophet of monotheism? Or was he a heretic who broke away from the broad, ancient ideological framework that kept Egypt great for millennia? Or was he simply an original thinker?

Most intriguing is his choice of this site for his new city. Was he truly unaware of the existence of Hermopolis and its significance? And if so, why did El-Armana, which was built on the eastern side of the Nile, have to extend its borders to the western side of the Nile to reach Tuna El-Gebel (Hermopolis West)? We cannot ignore Akhenaten's noted tolerance towards Thoth, who did not fall victim to persecution like other Egyptian deities. Or the exquisite statue depicting a scribe seated at the feet of a baboon-formed Thoth, which was recovered from the Amarna site and is now kept at the Cairo museum (Kemp 2011). Is it simply coincidence that, soon after Akhenaten's reign, we find Horemheb's famous *Hymn to Thoth*?

Perhaps more surprising, however, is the discovery of archæological evidence to support the involvement of Akhenaten's father, Amenhotep III, in the rebuilding of Thoth's temple in Ashmunin. On one of the statues at the Karnak temple depicting Amenhotep, son of Hapu (the favourite scribe at the time of Akhenaten's father), the following words are written: 'I was introduced to the divine books, I beheld the excellent things of Thoth and was equipped with their secrets' (Okinga 1986).

The link between Amarna and Hermopolis here is speculative and awaits further study and exploration. However, in *Akhenaten and the Religion of Light*, Hornung (2001) traces Akhenaten's 'solar ideology' to his father and predecessor,

Amenhotep III, and credits Akhenaten with making the *light* and not the sun the absolute reference point. This emphasis on the abstract notion of light—that which makes the hidden visible, and which 'gives life to what does not exist'—reveals a clear Hermetic sentiment (Quirke 2011).

The connection between Akhenaten's conceptual city and Hermetic thinking does not end here. We also see the involvement of Akhenaten in the Hermetic reformation movement of the Rosicrucians, where he became almost a revered prophet figure. This esoteric order, along with other movements, will be touched on in the next chapter, where Hermetic philosophy and its affiliated movements will be discussed.

It is clear from what has been said so far that what we could call a 'geo-Hermetica belt' extends beyond the boundaries of Hermopolis to include almost all the ancient sites within its vicinity. It is perhaps important to add that all the copies of *The Book of Two Ways* were found at Deir El-Bersha, where the rulers and scribes of Hermopolis in the Middle Kingdom were buried. They referred to themselves in this book, which was a precursor to the important *Book of the Dead*, as the 'genuine sons of Thoth' (Hornung 1999).

To the south of Hermopolis lies Lycopolis (Asyut), where Plotinus—generally regarded as the father of Neoplatonism—was born. Lycopolis was named after the Egyptian jackal- headed deity Wepwawet, who is often confused with the dog-headed Anubis. In Greek times, Wepwawet, whose name curiously translates as 'the opener of the ways', was combined with Hermes in the figure of Hermanubis, who is commonly portrayed holding the sacred Caduceus known to be associated with Hermes.

However, the term 'Hermetica belt' more commonly refers to Hermopolis, Panopolis (Akhmim), and Nag Hammadi. Nag Hammadi is well known for the library where the famous Gnostic and Hermetic scriptures were discovered in 1945. Panopolis (Akhmim), which lies between Hermopolis to the North and Nag Hammadi to the South, was incidentally named after Pan, the satyr poet who is commonly regarded as the son of Hermes. Panopolis is the city where the father of alchemy, Zosimus, was born, and is well-recognised for being an important Hermetic and alchemical centre, particularly in early Christian and Islamic Egypt.

Hermopolis and the genius loci

Hermopolis may therefore be defined as a geo-spiritual region of Egypt, a heritage city that has revealed itself from the very beginning as a space of harmony and creativity based upon a spiritual vision of humanity (Nasser 2009).

The genius loci, or 'spirit of place', has recently been put forward to refer to the unique, distinctive, and cherished aspects of any given site; the expression applies both to its tangible and intangible associative elements. Throughout the ages, the notion of the genius loci was essentially derived from the fact that particular areas of the world were occupied by gods or spirits who are worthy of reverence. These places are therefore regarded as places of homage or pilgrimage (Petzet 2009). It is interesting to note that as recently as the twentieth century, Hermopolis was mentioned in some Egyptian Arabic literature as the 'City of Pilgrimage'.

Hermopolis, therefore, is not only the city of the great figure of Hermes; it is also the city that was credited with generating a body of ideas that influenced many great minds across both centuries and nations.

The 'sense of place' in this meaningful landscape is mainly concerned with the interaction of our souls with the accumulated history of this location and its thought. It is the enigma of how this city managed to leave its imprint on our imagination and link our minds through its wisdom, regardless of who we are and where we come from:

> Wise words
> Although written by my decaying hand,
> Remain imperishable
> Through time...
> Until an older heaven
> Births human beings
> Who are worthy
> Of your wisdom.
> HERMETICA

*And you will realise they are united,
linked together, and connected
by the chain of Being.*

CORPUS HERMETICUM

II

MIGRATIONS
of the Hermetic Idea

The Hermetic notion of universal oneness

THE FOUNDING OF ALEXANDRIA, as discussed in the first chapter, was inspired by the cosmic nature of Hermopolis, in which all individuals could live and relate to one another regardless of country, race, or religion. The central idea of the *Hermetica* sees the universe as both one and all, while the human being—the microcosm—is seen to combine within itself all the powers and virtues of the natural world: the macrocosm around it:

> The Cosmos is One
> And so is man
> For like the Cosmos

He is a whole made up
Of different diverse parts.
HERMETICA

It is in this sense that Alexandria became the prime example of a *world-city*, and by the time of Alexander's successor, Ptolemy I, it also became the ultimate philosophical centre of the world. It had a great library that housed over half a million scrolls spanning all spheres of knowledge, and it produced some of the finest minds and achievements of the ancient world. Among them was Euclid, Archimedes, Herophilus, and the astronomer Ptolemy (Abadi 2002).

With the Roman rule of Egypt and subsequently the advent of Christianity, there was an urgent need to bring this Hermetic philosophy in line with the new creed. A major figure in this process was Clement of Alexandria, who was born in the second century CE. Truly conversant with the philosophies of the Hellenistic world, he taught his pupil Origen what he called 'faith of knowledge', which was by and large based on the Hermetic concept of the unity of knowledge (*gnōsis*). This unity of knowledge encompassed the self, the world, and the divine (Slavenburg 2012).

In the *City of God*, Augustine refers to Egypt as 'the temple of the entire world' and sees Hermes as the precursor of the Christian faith. The *Hermetica* therefore became a source of 'eternal philosophy' or *prisca theologia*, with an underlying core of truth—a true religion and philosophy that prevailed in the ancient world and was seen to predate Greek and Hebrew traditions (Slavenburg 2012).

The concept of oneness was further developed in Neoplatonic discourse. Central to Neoplatonism was the belief in the transcendental one from which the rest of the universe emanated through self-creation from the one. Neoplatonism was developed by Plotinus in Alexandria around the third century CE, however the term was only coined in the nineteenth century to highlight the philosophical differences between this doctrine and that of Plato.

With the contribution of significant proponents such as Porphyry, Iamblichus, and Proclus, Neoplatonism became a major intellectual force and attracted the fellowship of several Alexandrian philosophers around that time (Gregory 1999).

However, with the rise of intolerant strains of Christianity, particularly under the reign of Cyril, and the savage murder of the Neoplatonic philosopher and mathematician Hypatia (fourth century CE), this vibrant philosophical situation would soon decline (Dzielska 2002).

By the fifth century CE, scientists and philosophers were forced to leave Alexandria to escape religious persecution. Some went to Florence, Italy, and others to the newly emerging Arab Muslim world, taking with them their Hermetic knowledge and the memories of the golden age of Alexandria (Pollard & Reid 2006).

Hermetic pathways:
From Alexandria to the world

RENAISSANCE HERMETICISM:
THE BIRTH OF HUMANISM

In 1460 an Egyptian monk brought the Hermetic manuscripts that were collected in the city of Alexandria almost a
millennium earlier to the new Platonic Academy in Florence.
The Florentine academy was established by Cosimo de' Medici, the reigning king in all but name, and an important patron
of arts and learning. On seeing the manuscripts, the Medici
came to the conclusion that they were much older than Plato
and Moses, and ordered their immediate translation. The task
was entrusted to the classical scholar, Marsilio Ficino. Beautifully described as a 'friend of mankind', Ficino lived as he
taught, devoting his life to beauty, reconciliation, and unity
(Shepherd 1999).

Ficino gave the name *Poimanders*—the name of the first
treatise of the *Hermetica*—to his translation. While this term
has previously been translated as 'shepherd' or 'great mind',
more recent translations have defined it as the 'knowledge of
Ra' (*P-eime-nte Ra*) (Kingsley 1993; Slavenburg 2012). This
knowledge is the *gnōsis* that guides the solar bark of the god
Ra out of darkness to the safety of the shores. Whoever pos-
sesses this knowledge is also capable of finding divinity within
themselves.

FIGURE 7.

Bust of Marsilio Ficino by Andrea Ferrucci,
Santa Maria del Fiore (Cathedral of Florence).
(Sixteenth Century).

Ficino's translation had a profound influence on many of the major intellectual and artistic figures who were instrumental in determining the direction the Renaissance would take.

More importantly, however, was the impact that this translation had on the church, particularly its attitude towards classical philosophy, which helped them to find a reconciliatory path between Hermetic philosophy and Christianity. A testimony to this is the floor of Siena Cathedral, where the figure of Hermes Trismegistus is depicted holding his sacred scripture and flanked by two sibyls, as if prophesying the coming of Christ (Copenhaver 1992).

In the Hermetic teachings, man—the human being—is seen as a marvel with one purpose in life: to awaken his divine nature. This is the true meaning of the Humanism that has become the hallmark of Renaissance thinking, a philosophical system that sees the human being as the ultimate source of value and the measure of all things (Cassirer 1972).

Like Alexandria a thousand years earlier, Renaissance Italy viewed science, art, literature, and religion as part of a united whole to be studied together. All aspects of human life were open for investigation, and for this reason, the Hermetic circles in Italy included figures that played a significant role in the advancement of science.

One of the most significant of these was Giordano Bruno, who through his knowledge of the *Hermetica* was able to lend significant support to Copernicus' theory of the heliocentric nature of the cosmos. Bruno was in favour of reviving the ancient Hermetic spirit, and to pioneering a 'new age' that was both pluralistic and pantheistic. His ideas, however, put

FIGURE 8.

*Hermes Trismegistus depicted on the floor
of the Cathedral of Siena.*

him in direct conflict with the church, and as a result he was burned at the stake at the hands of the inquisition in Rome (Yates 1971).

With the advent of printing, Ficino's translation of the *Hermetica* was no longer limited to Italy. Before long, it became available and accessible in every corner of the European world (Cronin 1967; Ebeling 2007).

THE HOUSE OF WISDOM IN BAGHDAD: FROM SELF-ALCHEMY TO SUFISM

Several centuries before the Florentine Renaissance, another group of scholars and philosophers left Alexandria for the east. Their first destination was Harran in present day Turkey. They were known as Sabians, a name derived from a word meaning 'star' (in likely reference to their profound knowledge of astrology). The Sabians were instantly regarded as carriers of ancient knowledge, which helped make Harran an important centre of learning in the early Islamic world (Peters 1990).

Some of the Sabians of Harran later became members of the Brethern of Purity in Iraq, who were by and large behind the establishment of the famed House of Wisdom in Baghdad. The House of Wisdom was the pride of the golden age of Arabic science and culture that flourished between eighth and tenth centuries CE (Abadi 2002; El-Daly 2005).

The interest of the early Arab scholars in the *Hermetica* was huge, and they left us an imposing collection of Arabic Hermetic manuscripts (El-Daly 2005). However, their preference was more towards the medical and alchemical texts contained in the *Emerald Tablet* (*Tabula Smaragdina*), which the world came to know of through its first Arabic translation. In this text, the philosopher's stone is mentioned for the first time in history as the alchemical substance essential to turning base metals into gold: the first matter (*prima materia*) that is yet to exist, the very essence of the Hermopolitan creation (Slavenburg 2012).

The word alchemy is in fact derived from the ancient name for Egypt, *kemi*, meaning the 'black land' (with reference to its fertile soil). The Egyptian word became the basis of the Arabic word *al-kīmiyā*, or alchemy. The early Arab alchemists were heavily influenced by Zosimos, the 'father of alchemy' in Græco-Roman Egypt. Zosimos was closely associated with the city of Panopolis (Akhmim), which became an early centre for the alchemical arts and sciences (El-Daly 2005).

A mystical conception of alchemy, emphasising the connection between wisdom, transformation, and healing, was at the root of all Sufi traditions. The Hermetic mixing bowl of the mind (the *kratēr* of *nous*), discussed in the Greek *Hermetica*, highlighted the alchemical transmutation of the soul: the act of purifying and perfecting the *psyche* so that it could finally be lead to self-realisation (Lindsay 1970; Fowden 1986).

He filled a great bowl with Mind
and sent it down to Earth
Ascend to him who sent this bowl.
THE MIXING BOWL (HERMETICA)

Sufism began around the ninth century CE with another inhabitant of Akhmim, Dhūl-Nūn the Egyptian (Al-Misrī), an alchemist, physician, linguist, and Hermeticist who is commonly regarded as the first to introduce the concept of *gnōsis* into Islam. He had knowledge of the Egyptian hieroglyphs and believed they provided the keys to deciphering ancient Hermetic knowledge (Shepherd 2010).

Very little is known about Dhūl-Nūn's way of thinking, as scarcely any of his writings have survived. Most of what we know of his philosophy came to us almost three centuries later through the work of Muhyiddin Ibn 'Arabi (twenfth century CE). In his *Brilliant Star*, Ibn 'Arabi wrote about Dhūl-Nūn's life and teachings, as well as his unique spiritual path. In particular, he emphasised Dhūl-Nūn's concept of 'creative compassion', which provided a way for humanity to form compassionate ties with one another despite differences and diversity. This concept greatly influenced Ibn 'Arabi's formulation of his own 'religion of love', in which the *many*, despite their differences, are always able to be united in their relationship to the *one* (Twinch 2010):

> My heart now can take on any form:
> A meadow for gazelles,
> A cloister for monks,
> For the idols, sacred ground,
> Ka'ba for the circling pilgrim,
> The tables of the Torah,
> The scrolls of the Quran.
> My creed is Love;

Wherever its caravan turns along the way,
That is my belief,
My faith is love.

IBN ʿARABI

Almost a century later, the same sentiment was to find its expression in the poetic words of the great mystic, Jalāl ad-Dīn Rumi (thirteenth century CE):

On the seeker's path, wise men and fools are one.
In His love, brothers and strangers are one.
Go on! Drink the wine of the Beloved!
In that faith, Muslims and pagans are one.

RUMI

Both Ibn ʿArabi and Rumi are now considered to be the main pillars of Sufism. Together they provided a new vision for humanity in which the heart—as the ancient Egyptians always believed—was the seat of wisdom and love (Ibn ʿArabi Society 2013).

THE GERMAN-SPEAKING HERMES
AND FURTHER TALES OF TRANSFORMATION

In the twelfth century CE, the *Emerald Tablet* was translated into Latin and had a huge influence on the Renaissance of northern Europe, and in particular, Germany. The power of allegory in the alchemical journey of self-transformation was to direct the great German artist Albrecht Dürer (fifteenth century CE) to the symbolic power of the Egyptian language. This led him to suggest a form of Renaissance picture writing. Dürer's picture writing was envisioned as a new universal language and medium of communication, particularly between the learned people of the world (Hornung 2001).

However, the main proponent of this alchemical tradition in the German-speaking world was Paracelsus, the sixteenth century Swiss philosopher and physician who was declared the legitimate heir of the Egyptian Hermes.

Paracelsus advocated the notion of holistic medicine in the sense that he treated the human being as a whole in body and soul. In his work, the *Aurora of Philosophers*, he made several references to the *Emerald Tablet* and called Hermes the 'father of all philosophers'. Of alchemy, Paracelsus has said that 'the one who is fully accomplished in this Art, creates a new world' (Paracelsus 1967).

The true impact of Hermeticism on the German mind did not reach its peak until the eighteenth century, with the great age of German Romanticism. Goethe, who is generally regarded as Germany's greatest man of letters, began to study Hermetic literature and alchemy at an early age, and much of what he learned from these sources found a place in his works *Faust* and *Tales for Transformation*.

Goethe's *Faust* is now considered as one of the pillars of world literature (*Weltliteratur*), a term that was introduced by Goethe himself to acknowledge the contribution of ancient literary sources in his work and the relevance of the diversity of sources to all intellectual creations of humanity. As for his

FIGURE 9.

1. *Theophrastus Bombastus von Hohenheim (Paracelsus);*
2. *Dr. John Dee;* 3. *Johann Wolfgang von Goethe;*
4. *Friedrich Schiller.*

Tales for Transformation, we see in this work an abundance of alchemical symbolism revolving around self-mastery and self-renewal. The *Tales* expand on the theme of art, creativity, and human genius, particularly the power of music in any journey for self-transformation. This was clearly shown in Goethe's sequel to Mozart's *Magic Flute*, which was inspired by the Hermetic enlightenment in which music was seen as a creative weapon in humanity's eternal struggle between forces of darkness and light (Slavenburg 2012).

The same impact is also seen in Schiller's poetry (1795), particularly his poem 'The Veiled Image of Sais', which was supposedly based on the inscription in the temple of Isis at Sais, with its reference to the 'veiled light of truth' and humanity's quest to lift this veil in its eternal pursuit of knowledge (Hornung 2001):

> I am what is, and what will be, and what has been,
> No one has lifted my veil.
> The fruit I bore was the sun.
> SCHILLER

THE ENGLISH ELIZABETHAN COURT, THE NEW WORLD, AND THE BIRTH OF UTOPIANISM

The story for England was somewhat different, as it was initially influenced by the Italian Renaissance, which spread rapidly in the English royal courts. Historians argue that Thomas

More's *Utopia* was inspired by Hermetic humanism, particularly its emphasis on the idea of religious freedom.

FIGURE 10.

John Dee's Monas Hieroglyphica, an emblem demonstrating the unity of solar, lunar, & elemental principles.

The availability of the Hermetic texts in Elizabethan England kindled the desire for learning and had an impact on major English figures such as William Shakespeare, Francis Bacon, and the mathematician-philosopher, Dr. John Dee, who was the first to translate the complete works of Euclid into English. His alchemical knowledge was behind his invention of the Hermetic seal known as the *monas hieroglyphica*, a composite symbol that was designed to represent the unity of the entirety of existence, very much like Dee's own library (which was seen to embrace the whole universe to the extent that it rivalled the great libraries of Oxford and Cambridge at that time) (French 1972; Slavenburg 2012).

This enlightened Elizabethan age continued to have its influence on other scholarly figures such as Francis Bacon, whose book, *The New Atlantis*, is considered the blueprint for the creation of the New American Republic (Dawkins 1984).

Emerson, the nineteenth-century American Philosopher who is commonly referred to as the prophet of American idealism, realised that the seeds of future thought were to be found in ancient wisdom. He believed that life-force was a force for good, a life-force that lies within an 'all embracing soul' that holds the key to a better and more humane world (Emerson & Needleman 2008).

HERMETIC FRATERNITY

Throughout history, Hermetic philosophy had both proponents and opponents, almost in equal measures. It received a major blow, however, in the early part of the seventeenth century with the Swiss scholar Isaac Casaubon, who waged a war against it. Casaubon regarded the *Hermetica* as a mere Christian forgery, claiming that it was possibly used by the early pious Christians to give authority to their new religion in order to help them convert more pagans to the new faith (Ebeling 2007).

Casaubon arrived at a time when Europe was embroiled in the split between Catholicism and the Protestant Reformation. In this climate, discrediting Hermeticism was considered a way of resisting the new wave of religious reform. However, he could not deny the existence of a real Hermes Trismegistus or the idea of a *prisca theologia* that is rooted in ancient Egyptian wisdom (Lachman 2011).

The only thing that Casaubon's attack did was to drive the Hermetic tradition and its thinkers underground. This resulted in the formation of several secret societies, among which was the fraternity of the Rosy Cross—the Rosicrucians—whose origin remains a mystery. The movement is generally believed to have begun in Germany as part of the religious reform movement. Their documents, which are known to us today as manifestos, speak of a universal reformation of mankind and world renewal, involving religion, society, art, and politics, which were to a large extent based on the science of alchemy and the ancient Hermetic wisdom.

The Rosicrucians spread to the rest of Europe and then to America. The American order that was established in the twentieth century traced its beginnings to the seventeenth century, and even saw its origin to go back to ancient Egypt and to Akhenaten's new religion, whose city, as mentioned before, lies within the geographical remit of ancient Hermopolis (Yates 1972; Hornung 2001).

The Rosicrucian movement was also thought to be behind the foundation of English Freemasonry, which also integrated medieval traditions such as the Knights Templar, with whom they shared their reverence for the legendary Temple of Solomon, with all its connotative associations of wisdom (Lachman 2011). The Freemasons were initially formed as a human fraternity with an aim to transcend national politics and international boundaries in order to pursue man's spiritual and moral elevation. They had a core belief in a super-being

FIGURE 11.

*The Tabula Smaragdina, or 'Emerald Tablet of Hermes Trismegistus',
as depicted in Heinrich Khunrath's 'Ampitheatrum Sapientiæ Æternæ'
(Ampitheater of Eternal Wisdom, 1595). A translation from the Latin
by Isaac Newton appears on the following page.*

TIS TRUE WITHOUT LYING, certain and most true.
That which is below is like that which is above
and that which is above is like that which is below
to do the miracles of one only thing
And as all things have been and arose from one by the mediation of one:
so all things have their birth from this one thing by adaptation.

The Sun is its father,
the moon its mother,
the wind hath carried it in its belly,
the earth is its nurse.
The father of all perfection in the whole world is here.
Its force or power is entire if it be converted into earth.

Separate thou the earth from the fire,
the subtle from the gross
sweetly with great industry.
It ascends from the earth to the heaven
and again it descends to the earth
and receives the force of things superior and inferior.
By this means you shall have the glory of the whole world
and thereby all obscurity shall fly from you.

Its force is above all force.
For it vanquishes every subtle thing and penetrates every solid thing.
So was ye world created.
From this are and do come admirable adaptations
where of the means is here in this.

Hence I am called Hermes Trismegist,
having the three parts of the philosophy of the whole world
That which I have said of the operation of the Sun
is accomplished and ended.

THE EMERALD TABLET
OF HERMES TRISMEGISTUS

understood as the great architect of the universe, regardless of individual religions. This was behind their fascination with the Temple of Solomon, which was regarded as the epitome of age-old geometric principles and sacred mathematical measurements, like the Temple of Thoth that once stood in Hermopolis (Hamblin & Seely 2007).

Several other spiritual and esoteric movements with links to Rosicrucianism and Freemasonry sprang up in Europe and America throughout the eighteenth and nineteenth centuries. The most significant of all was the Theosophical Society, which was established in New York in 1875. The principal woman behind it was the influential Russian occultist, Helena Petrovna Blavatsky, who made her fame through the publication of two major books: *Isis Unveiled* (1877) and *The Secret Doctrine* (1888). The Theosophical Society was largely based on the idea of universal brotherhood without distinction of race, belief, sex, caste, or colour. Among its main aims were the study of comparative religion, the investigation of the unexplained laws of nature, and the exploration of latent human potential (Faivre 2000).

The Theosophical Society gave birth to a number of groups that called themselves Hermetic Orders, including the Brotherhood of Luxor and the Golden Dawn, which included the literary giant, W. B. Yeats, among its notable members (Godwin 1995; Wasserman 2005).

THE HERMETIC TERTIUM NON DATUR

The appeal of the Hermetic Idea clearly lies in its emphasis on the unity of humanity, the harmonious order of the universe, and the potential of the human being to ascend to higher planes and transform itself and its world through its creative mind. It seems to be always present when we think of concepts such as Humanism, Idealism, Utopianism, and Fraternity: ideals that we can all cherish and stand for, and which remain the substance of our dreams for a better world.

The expression *tertium non datur* (literally: third not given) was used by Umberto Eco (1990) to describe the Hermetic Idea as a reconciliatory third way that carries the possibility of bringing the whole world together despite its diversity. However, it comes into direct contradiction with our upheld rationality and its logic of the 'excluded middle'. Whereas the logic of the excluded middle held that something either *is* or *is not* true, the *tertium non datur* is based on an entirely different type of reason: a syncretistic one that enables us to think of a *coincidence of opposites* in which difference and contradiction can be integrated into what we are familiar with (Eco 1990).

With this approach, we can hope to gain a better understanding of the interface between the human mind and the rich reservoir of ideas within the human psyche. From this, we can possibly learn to resolve some of our vexed conflicts about the issue of otherness.

This approach can be seen in the significant works of William James (1902) and Carl Gustav Jung (1968), both of whom were influenced by the Hermetic Idea. Both were able to see that the conflicting divisions of our world today mirroring the psychological chaos within our souls. To resolve these divisions, we need to learn how to reconcile and integrate those chaotic fragments in order to achieve the cohesion and oneness of the Self. The contribution of the Hermetic Idea to the field of human psychology will be discussed in more detail in the following chapter.

The history of Hermes and his thought seems, as Slavenburg said, to be our history (Slavenburg 2012). It answers questions about where we came from, who we are, and what the future will be. It also predicts the same unfortunate story when we give in to dogma and rigid thought; yet it forces its light through our conscience at times when we are shrouded in darkness. It is quite simply the hope we have in our troubled times. As Yeats remarks in 'Blood and the Moon':

> Alexandria was a beacon tower,
> And Babylon's
> An image of the moving heaven
> A log book of the sun's journey
> And the moon ...
> I declare this tower is my
> Symbol, I declare
> This winding, gyring, spinning treadmill
> Of stairs is my ancestral stair.
> YEATS

In the waters of potentiality,
exists the first principles
of all in the universe.

CORPUS HERMETICUM

III

HERMETICISM

as a Philosophy of Hope

What is hope?

ACCORDING TO YET ANOTHER myth of creation from ancient Hermopolis, a grand lotus emerged out of the primitive, chaotic, muddy waters; when its blossoms opened it revealed the sun. At sunset, the lotus closed its petals and sunk back under the water and would resurface with the rising of the sun. As such it symbolised life's perpetual beginnings and renewals.

Being for the Egyptians was no different from that lotus which opens with the sunrise and sinks with the sunset. Like *death resurrected*, new life springs from the inertness and hiddenness. What this meant was that that the *act of being* was never separate from *non-being*, and that creation was never a one-off incident, but something that entailed constant repetition. *Being* and the *creating of being* were one and the same thing, often described as the condition 'when there were not yet two things' and 'when strife has not yet existed', pointing to the constant struggle entailed in the act of becoming within being (Hornung 1992):

> I was alone with the primeval Ocean, in the inertness. Floating between (two) waters, totally inert ... and it was my son, *life*, that roused my spirit, who made my heart live and gathered up my inert members.
> COFFIN TEXTS (Faulkner 2007)

In his *Principle of Hope*, Ernst Bloch (1995) regarded the state of 'not-yet-being' as an essential pre-requisite for hope. He saw us as creatures living in the future and always striving past the present moment. This future orientation tends to negate the present and make our existence one of constant motion towards something beyond the present. Something we call *hope*, the most authentic of all human feelings, and known to be the only antidote to fear, anxiety, despair, and waiting:

> The emotion of hope requires people who throw themselves actively into what is becoming, to which they themselves belong.
> BLOCH (1986)

Bloch is one of the great twentieth century philosophers and is often described as a 'utopian thinker' or a 'poet of light' who urges us to see the past as illuminating the present, directing us towards a better future. History for him does not tell us only about the past, but it also provides the tools for restructuring the present, not from scratch nor from a point outside of it, but from within its ongoing process.

Bloch regards history as a 'repository of possibilities' that represent 'living options' for future action. Those options should help us to realise the unrealised potentialities that are latent in the present and which orient our present towards the direction of the future. Bloch referred to this as a state of 'anticipatory consciousness' that allows us to grasp at once the emancipatory potential that lies in the past, the latencies and tendencies of our present time and the realisable hopes of the future (Bloch 1995).

> The present issues from the past,
> and the future from the present.
> Everything is made one
> by this continuity.
> HERMETICA

Bloch believed that we (as humanity) carry enough good future in our historical baggage, which he saw as a surplus of utopian thought that goes back to ancient philosophers. This surplus of past good thought should equip us to think forward and engage in a future that could make humanity's deepest dreams possible (Bloch 1995).

The Hermetic promise

So, through philosophy,
they might nurture men's souls
And cure sickness of the body
with the healing arts.

HERMETICA

Hermeticism is a philosophical system based on the study of the *Hermetica* as a way of helping the soul (*psychē*) to develop reasonable mind (*nous*), reasonable speech (*logos*), and self-knowledge (*gnōsis*), so we may begin to understand the world and our place in it.

The *Hermetica* are written in a poetic style, full of aphorisms. It takes the form of dialogues between teacher and pupil or father and son. They are not dissimilar to the Platonic dialogues, which may have been inspired by the dialogical form of the original Egyptian texts. They stimulate reflection and seldom provide prescriptive answers, but encourage instead the use of one's mind to probe deep beneath the surface to find meaning for our existence and new paths for self-realisation. In the words of Clement Salman (2007), 'there are passages in Hermes which may be read in a few seconds and yet contemplated for life'.

The human being lies at the very centre of the Hermetic worldview; it is believed that the individual human harbours the seeds of all possibilities that grow from every form of life. Through this, humankind has the power to shape the universe. And, the universe of the *Hermetica* is not static, but ever-changing, revolving, and evolving, constantly governed by the process of turning and returning. *Time* acts as the regulator of this change, which in turn is measured by the recurring cycles of the stars and the sun, which revolve in fixed and permanent orbits. All of which eventually bring things back to where they started, for cyclic time has neither beginning nor end (Freke & Gandy 1999).

[They] transform everything
according to the law of natural growth,
creating from the permanent unchanging Reality,
a permanently changing world.
HERMETICA

The Hermetic universe is also regarded as an open-ended and allegorical one, making the world, in Eco's words, a 'linguistic theatre', which gives us the freedom of infinite interpretation and interconnection. It is no surprise therefore to find that the science of hermenutics was actually derived from the *Hermetica* (Eco 1990).

In this wide universe with its rich symbols and metaphors, we find that opposites coincide, allowing the self to have an inner dialectic with its opposing forces, which helps its continual growth and development towards a better, more perfected self (Lineman, 1993). This journey towards an integrated and harmonious whole agrees with what Plimer (2014) described as the 'Hermetic meditation on the Highest Good'. This all-embracing whole is described in the *Hermetica* as follows:

Make yourself higher than the highest
and deeper than the depths.
Embrace within yourself all opposites
heat and cold, hard and fluid ...
Imagine yourself unborn in the womb,
yet also old, and already dead,
in the world beyond the grave.

HERMETICA

In his book *The Quest for Hermes Trismegistus*, Lachman (2011) referred to Hermeticism as the religion of the mind, a perfect description for an intellectual discourse that clearly speaks to our psyches and gives us the necessary tools to be truly human. It is no exaggeration to say that it is a blueprint of what we came to know in our modern time as Humanistic Psychology. The *Hermetica* may be seen to clearly espouse the following humanistic principles:

1. The power of the human creative potential.
2. The necessity of integrating opposing forces within one's self to achieve wholeness.
3. The realisation of the ever-changing, ever-evolving nature of the universe that is described as a linguistic phenomenon with multiple interpretations and a variety of discourses.
4. The acknowledgment of the connection between the universal and the particular.

The Hermetic pioneers
of existence

> The act of being is a progressive task
> towards pioneering existence.
> BLOCH (1995)

Ernst Bloch and Walter Benjamin are two German intellec-
tuals that belong to the generation that was caught between
the nightmares of two World Wars. Benjamin saw history as
a redeemer, an 'angel of history' that restores what has been
smashed—making it whole again through a new acquired understanding. He believed that every history has a new afterlife
in the realm of the mind that entails acts of renovation, a revival and a reconstruction where our living process generates
new meanings from their historical roots or seeds. This phenomenon was referred to by the German concept of *Nachle-
ben*, or 'life after life', which is clearly seen in the case of any
'living antiquity'.

According to Benjamin, the way we read, translate, and
interpret history and its artefacts tend to survive their original forms by being taken into our consciousness to a much
higher realm. Our minds perceive history as an undiscovered
continent of possibilities that awaits our exploration and our
utopian intention for further fulfillment (Benjamin 2009).

Pioneering existence thus requires us to activate the ten-
dency inherent in history and which proceeds dialectically, in-
augurating a new relationship between the ego and the world
(Bloch 1995). And this is the case of the pioneers that we are

FIGURE 12.

1. *William James; 2. Ernst Bloch;*
3. *Walter Benjamin; 4. Viktor Frankl.*

about to discuss, who, through their creative perception of the Hermetic philosophy, managed to venture into new ways of understanding the self in relation to others, time, and the universe. All of these pioneers saw history as a well of ideas filled with intellectual provocations towards new and unlimited creations.

MULTIPLICITY OF THE SELF
AND THE UNITY OF BEING

The All is not many separate things,
but the Oneness that subsumes the parts.
HERMETICA

William James is one of the greatest minds in American psychology and philosophy in the late nineteenth and early twentieth century. His major works include *The Principles of Psychology* (1890), *Varieties of Religious Experience* (1902), and *A Pluralistic Universe* (1909). He considered philosophy to be a major contributor to establishing 'overbeliefs' regarding the existence and nature of the divine. He saw life as an evolutionary task towards achieving happiness, which he believed to be determined to a large extent by the way we act to make our life better.

In his book, *The Principles of Psychology*, James made a clear distinction between two aspects of the self: the self as a subject or the 'I' and the self as an object or the 'me'. This 'me' is the empirical self, that is material (body and possessions),

social (friends, relatives, culture), and spiritual (ideas and belief system). The 'I', on the other hand, is the transcended self
which does the knowing; it is the pure ego that is immaterial
and identifiable with the soul. According to James, 'Selfhood'
is conceived as a product of a dialogue between the 'I' and the
other in 'me', resulting in the many 'I' positions that can be
occupied by the same person.

The term 'dialogical self' was first coined by H. J. M. Herman (2001) to refer precisely to this dynamic multiplicity of
the Self, namely the 'I' position(s) in relation to the multiple
'me's in a multi-voiced interiority of the Self. This paradigm
is borrowed from literature, particularly Bakhtin's theory of
the Self as a 'polyphonic narrative' in which the 'I' acts as the
author and the 'me' as the protagonist. The 'I' fluctuates along
different and sometimes opposed positions that are metaphorically endowed with voices that allow for such dialogical
interaction. The linguistic text on the other hand acts as a 'dic-
tionary of the soul' open for reflection, and for the creation
of metamorphic or alternative beings (Bakhtin 1973; Herman
2001). This is relevant in the context of our present techno-
logical self, where the new 'extended self' is now in constant
dialogue between its core self and the numerous selves that are
encountered in the virtual domain.

The dialogue of the self with the self is not only limited
to various textual selves, it also takes place between the self (or
selves) and time. That is, it occurs via the engagement of the
present self with its past and future selves. The present self is
always open to the future in its quest to achieve a 'purposive
existence', which requires the synthesis, cohesion, and integra-

tion of the self and its own multiplicity in order to achieve the 'totality of the self'—or what James beautifully described as 'the sum of what a man *can* call his'.

This, in a nutshell, is the essence of James' philosophy, which he called the 'Mind-Cure Movement'. Here, the diversity of the self is regarded as the default state of any human situation, and for an individual to live in harmony, they need to perform an 'inner marriage' between their different mosaic parts. This marriage is performed to bring about the synthesis of its multiplicity, and to realise what makes the person truly unique (James 2013).

THE UNDISCOVERED SELF:
HERMETIC POTENTIALITIES

> The human race, for example, shares a common universal form by which we know that a man is a man. Yet all human beings have a distinctly different particular form, of which no two are entirely alike
> HERMETICA

What was said above about William James can also be said here about Carl Jung, whose book, *Psychology and Alchemy*, clearly states that the balanced or harmonised self cannot be achieved other than through the integration of the conscious and unconscious or chaotic parts of the self (Jung 1968).

Jung is one of psychiatry's greatest minds, and perhaps one of the most Hermetic and Gnostic of all the thinkers discussed here. He wrote about the Hermetic and Nag Hammadi scriptures, the Visions of Zosimos, and the influence that Paracelsus and Goethe had on him. Jung is known as a psychodynamic analyst famous for his theories of the archetypes and the collective unconscious. However the Jung I wish to discuss here is the existential one: the psychologist of human potentialities and true becoming.

> I am not what happened to me,
> I am what I choose to become.
> C. G. JUNG

In his book, *The Undiscovered Self* (2006), he makes a plea to the Self to know itself, because for Jung, our very future depends on resisting the herd identity, and in differentiating our own self-values from the collective and mass cultural values.

The act of *individuation* can never be achieved without the Self's full knowledge of its opposing parts. Becoming *whole* is achieved precisely through the integration and harmonisation of these conflicting, polarised aspects. Only then can the Self discover its embedded potentials and pioneer an alternative existence.

It is important, however, to say that the process of individuation here should not be mistaken for cultivating individualistic or narcissistic streaks, or separating oneself from the collective society. The aim here is for the Self to see itself with the 'eye of the soul', to learn what genuinely belongs to it, and to achieve authenticity.

FIGURE 13.

1. *Rainer Maria Rilke;* 2. *Ruldolf Steiner;*
3. *Carl Gustav Jung;* 4. *Jean Gebser.*

THE SELF AND THE INTEGRAL CONSCIOUSNESS

> Think yourself everywhere at once,
> on land, at sea, in heaven ...
> Grasp in your mind all this at once,
> all times and places,
> all substances and qualities together.
>
> HERMETICA

Jean Gebser was a twentienth century Swiss poet, evolution-ary philosopher, and cultural historian who until recently was largely ignored by the academic world. This could possibly be due to the fact that he used new vocabulary in his work, and acknowledged his strong connection with spiritualism.

Gebser was perhaps the first thinker in our modern times to realise that our linear understanding of time was no lon-ger viable, and that the existing mental-rational structure of our consciousness was falling apart. In his outstanding book *The Ever-Present Origin*, which was published in English for the first time in 1986, Gebser spoke of a series of mutations that human consciousness underwent throughout history. According to Gebser, human consciousness began with the archaic, pre-dimensional structure, evolving into the magi-cal, mono-dimensional structure, followed by the mythical, two-dimensional structure, before reaching the rational, three dimensional structure, which currently dominates despite being deficient in coping with the demands of our times. Gebser proposed that we were on the cusp of a new mutation, which he called the *integral structure of consciousness*, which incorporates rationalality, but also integrates all the previous mutations of our consciousness. He believed that this new consciousness was capable of grasping both linear and cyclical approaches to time, and was able to embrace all aspects of life, such as myth, feelings, empathy, and more importantly, ego-transcendence, which he regarded as the decisive task of human life.

He referred to this new consciousness as *arational* (i.e., 'free from rationality', as distinguished from the irrational and the rational) and *aperspectival* (i.e., 'free from the perspectival', as distinguished from the non-perspectival and the perspectival). For Gebser, the arational consciousness enables us to transcend the dualistic dichotomies that characterise our present rational orientation.

Gebser's new consciousness should be able to take in the past, present, and future not as separate notions but as an integrating time structure, while engaging with the pluralistic spaces that make up our current world. However, this new consciousness should not be seen as an *evolution* but as an *integration*. It is an awareness that leads to the continual unfoldment of our hidden, potential abilities in order to bring us closer to the *all* mind, namely: moving from our limited mind to the super-mind.

In this process we are not required to surrender our ego as such, but to free ourselves from its limitations. By transcending the limited perspective of our current 'small self', which is aware of little more than appetites and complaints, we gain instead a 'bird's-eye-view' of the wider world beyond ourselves (Lachman 2015).

LIVING THROUGH THE MIND:
LOGOTHERAPY

> Listen every human heart, immerse yourself in Mind
> and recognize the purpose of your birth.
> HERMETICA

Logotherapy is a psychotherapeutic technique that was ini-
tiated by the Viennese existential psychiatrist, Victor Frankl.
It revolves around two Hermetic and Gnostic concepts, *logos*
(word) and *nous* (mind). Frankl used the word *logos* here as
'meaning', and *noetic* to point to an individual's 'spirituality',
particularly one that reflects everything that is essentially human. It includes ideas and ideals, imagination, self-transcendence, faith, love, and the freedom to make responsible choices. The principles of logotherapy are outlined in his book,
Man's Search for Meaning (2006), originally published in 1959
under the title: *From Death Camp to Existentialism*. The principles can be summed up in three requirements:

1. A task through which we are able to transcend
    ourselves.
2. A deep experience of a person or something such
    as love.
3. The attitude we take towards unavoidable suffer-
    ing.

According to Frankl, we all have an innate need to understand the world we live in and to search for a meaning that de-

mands our attention, action, and devotion. However, this primary motivation may lie dormant when we are preoccupied with success and the pursuit of happiness, *until* we are faced with a life crisis—personal or societal—that calls for meaning. This is very much in keeping with Albert Camus' remark that 'there is no love of life without despair of life' (1970).

Through self-transcendence, the focus of the Self is redirected from the personal impact of the crisis and its accustomed self-interest to something much bigger than the self, or even beyond the self, which enables us to experience the full range of our humanness and to find meaningful existence.

Frankl's emphasis on self-transcendence in response to our spiritual need for meaning is almost synonymous with the calling of the individual to discover their life-role through the use of their unique talents and experiences. This sense of calling endows one's life not only with hope and meaning, but responsibility and dignity.

Frankl noted that the people who were able to survive traumatic experiences in their lives were the ones who saw in them a meaning related to a task they needed to fulfill. This was clearly borne out by his suffering in the Nazi concentration camps. The suffering here is defined as the inevitable kind that one feels helpless in the face of. However, it is the *response* to this kind of unavoidable suffering that defines the free individual. Our ultimate freedom, as Frankl sees it, lies in the choices we make or the attitude we take in response to this unavoidable suffering. In Frankl's own words: 'A man who becomes conscious of the responsibility he bears toward a human being who affectionately waits for him, or to an unfinished work, will never be able to throw away his life. He knows the "why" for his existence and will be able to bear almost any "how".

THE SELF AS 'SOUL' AND 'SOIL'

> He raises reverent eyes to heaven above,
> and tends to earth below.
> He is blessed by being the intermediary.
> HERMETICA

It has often been said that Hermeticism has a specifically *green* form of spirituality—a sacred theory of earth (and by extension the human body). The *Emerald Tablet* is green and sees the self and the world as reflections of each other, as microcosm and macrocosm, or 'as above, so below' (Wilson 2007; Bamford 2007). This resonates beautifully with Goethe's words, attesting to his status as one of the greatest masters of Hermetic-Romantic science:

> When contemplating nature
> Always attend to the one and to the all:
> Nothing is within and nothing is without,
> What is inside is outside.
> GOETHE

Green Hermeticism is seen as a truly holistic science that transcends and erases all separations such as inner and outer, spirit and matter, divine and human, earthly and humanly. In the words of one of its great proponents, Christopher Bamford (2007), it is paradoxically 'primordial' and 'postmodern'.

The science of the greening of the soul seems to have its roots in a little-known work by the German poet Novalis (1772–1801). Entitled *The Novices at Sais*, Novalis' poem was inspired by Schiller's poem, 'The Veiled Image of Sais' (1795). Novalis believed in the power of imagination and the strong unity between the spiritual and the natural world. Commonly described as the most openly Hermetic of all the Romantics, Novalis' poetry is a transcendental journey towards a profound spiritual insight (Novalis 2005; Lachman 2011).

His unique insight is echoed in the work of one of the greatest poets of our modern era, Rainer Maria Rilke. Rilke believed that we need to transfer the outer world into our inner, invisible world. On one hand, this was to protect it from becoming 'meaningless', and on the other, it enabled us to germinate a new future world:

> Our task is to stamp this provisional perishing earth
> into ourselves so deeply, so painfully that its being
> may arise again invisibly in us, we are the bees of the
> invisible. RILKE (1939)

According to Rilke, we don't simply do this for ourselves, but as an effort on behalf of the *whole*, which enables us to become true players in the construction of our universe, and to fulfill our role as caretakers of the cosmos (Lachman 2011).

This poetic eco-spirituality was to find unique expression and new life in the work of the twentieth century Austrian philosopher and social reformer, Rudolf Steiner. Heavily influenced by Goethe, Steiner emerged from the Theosophical milieu, but eventually broke with it in order to establish Anthroposophy, which he conceived as a spiritual science. Steiner believed that *thinking* could be a spiritual path, aiming to sharpen the imaginative and the intuitive faculties of the individual (Lachman 2007).

Steiner's approach became highly influential, and resulted in several modern movements that believed in the possibility of a new social organism which could be developed through ecology and through an extended definition of art. Examples include Social Sculpture (Sacks 2011), Trans4m (www.trans-4-m.com), and Human Emergence (www.humanemergence.org). All of these movements see the Self as part of a larger, conscious whole.

Modern ecological movements such as these offer a new bio-psycho-social perspective on human living systems, a perspective that attempts to understand the current problems facing humanity and to find new solutions that are both hope-inspiring and life-affirming:

> In the past, changing the self and changing the world were often regarded as separate endeavors and viewed in either-or terms. But in the story of the Great Turning, they are recognised as mutually reinforcing and essential to one another.
>
> MACY & JOHNSTONE (2012)

Towards an old/new self

The end of becoming
is the beginning of destruction.
The end of destruction
is the beginning of becoming.

HERMETICA

This chapter began with the notion of *hope*, and discussed some of the philosophical and psychological pioneers whose work resonates deeply with our Hermetic roots. Ordinary hope is understood as the belief or trust in the potential of time, and in the good that tomorrow might bring. Hermetic hope, on the other hand, is the belief in the unlimited potenttial of the human being; the trust in its ability to always find a way towards a better future.

The past is perennial and forms a rich source of ideas if we would only revisit it with new eyes and fresh understanding. The past is also full of *tales of survival*, and many lessons on the art of *becoming within being* that can never be achieved unless we learn how to transcend our existing ego and replace it with a new Self. Above all, this new Self needs to be an integral Self that is capable of exploring the fullness of its potentialities and embracing its multiplicities. A new purposeful Self lives through *meaning*, and considers itself a part of this universe, connected to everything within it.

Although it might sound like a cliché, it is nevertheless vital to remind ourselves that by 'becoming the change we want to see', we can create the possibility of changing the world:

We row forward looking back, and telling this history is part of helping people navigate toward the future. We need a litany, a rosary, a sutra, a mantra, a war chant for our victories. The past is set in daylight, and it can become a torch we can carry into the night that is the future.

SOLNIT (2016)

I put the temple of Thoth
in its former condition
I made splendid what was ruined
I restored what had decayed long ago
and was no longer in its place.

PETOSIRIS

IV

REVIVAL

The Founding of the
New Hermopolis

Why me and why now?

SHE 'WHO RETRIEVED WHAT WAS LOST', she 'who res-
cued what was robbed', she 'who made what is'. These are all
descriptions of Nehmataway, one of the three major female
consorts that in the late period came to be associated with
Thoth. The other two are Maat, the symbol of truth and jus-
tice, and Seshat, the lady of writing who dwells in the house of
books (Boylan 1922; Bleeker 1973).

Inspired by those great women of ancient Hermopolis,
and following in the footsteps of its main scribe Petosiris, I
began in earnest to follow my quest to retrieve the lost soul of
Egypt and to revive the city where it lies.

New Hermopolis is an attempt to capture this lost soul without pretending in any way to imitate the grandeur of its past incarnation. It has in fact little to do with the actual monument, but through reviving its ancient spirit, we hope to highlight its significance and increase awareness of the need to protect it.

This project is designed to harness the ancient heritage of this city—both tangible and intangible—towards the cultural and economic development of its rural neighbourhood. It is an attempt to marry what we normally regard as abstract and sublime with what is mundane and concrete: to link the spiritual with the practical, the past with the present.

New Hermopolis lies within walking distance from Hermopolis West at Tuna El-Gebel, approximately 320 kilometres from Cairo. It serves the main city of Mallawi with its surrounding villages (twenty-four major villages, each with a population of around thirty thousand). Based on local government figures, this area exhibits some of the highest levels of poverty and marginalisation in the country. Despite its wealth of ancient culture, this land—once a great centre for learning and cultural dialogue—has since become impoverished and disregarded. Economic opportunities are scarce, but opportunities for free and critical thought are even scarcer; religious intolerance and needless strife, particularly along the Christian-Muslim juxtaposition, ranks higher in this region than in any other part of Egypt.

The idea for such a project had been in my mind since the early 1980s. It emerged in response to the growing wave of religious extremism that swept the country and made the

Egypt of my childhood unrecognisable. Many factors were behind this tragic phenomenon—political, economic, educational—but in my opinion, the single-most important reason was the almost complete dissociation of the Egyptians from their ancient past.

I felt a strong need to do something about this even if it sounded extremely naïve. Initially I began writing cultural critiques and essays discussing the situation, and they were luckily published in some Egyptian papers at the time. This was followed by a series of illustrated books on ancient Egypt that I wrote in Arabic, and which were specifically addressed to the young Egyptian reader (Nasser 2004).

However, as expected, and despite receiving an award for my children's Egyptology books, the impact of this writing effort was almost negligible. The circumstances also started to worsen: there were reports of book burnings, theatres being demolished, as well as attacks on writers, thinkers, and tourists. The situation, I felt, called for a greater response, a response that might have the power—even in a very small way—to counteract such a dark climate.

The years I spent studying ancient Egyptian history alongside my job as a psychiatrist in England directed me more towards the *mentality* behind those great Egyptian monuments, which eventually led me to Hermopolis and its underpinning philosophy. The idea of reviving such an ancient seat of harmony, tolerance, and dialogue seemed to me to be the correct response, even if, once again, it appeared naïve and imaginary.

My vision for the project was somewhat crystallised with the turning of the new millennium, when I began to feel ready to take the first practical steps. After a thorough study of the region, its people, its antiquities, and its existing facilities, I chose the desert side of the village of Tuna El-Gebel as the most appropriate site.

Although I made several attempts to work on this project in collaboration with the Egyptian authorities, unfortunately my efforts in this respect were in vain. This informed my decision to undertake the whole project by myself, which meant purchasing the land and securing the funds needed for such an exercise independently. This process required me to sell almost everything I own.

The search for a suitable piece of land in the chosen territory was by no means easy. The land in this area has disputed ownership, and its proximity to an antiquities site required clearance from the ministry of antiquities, which entailed dealing with bureaucratic issues, obstructive delays, and poor performance by local government officials.

After three years of searching, the land was secured. But it was nothing more than a barren desert with no water or energy supply, which necessitated the digging of a well as an essential first step. My desire to build in stone meant that the building materials and the skilled labourers had to be obtained from Fayoum, which is almost 150 kilometres from the project's location. This was due to the closure of the local quarry and the absence of stonemasons in the area. Regrettably, building in stone has become a dying skill like many other traditional trades in Egypt today.

Despite these difficulties, we were set for construction in 2007. At this time, I took complete retirement from my post as a consultant psychiatrist and senior university academic in England in order to dedicate myself entirely to this grand project. Since then I have spared no physical, financial, or emotional effort to try to make a success out of it.

The project was officially opened in December 2011. At the time, Egypt was caught up in the wider political turmoil and instability affecting the whole Middle East. No words can better articulate the chaos and disarray that we suffered more poignantly than the words of Petosiris, when he described the situation of Egypt in ancient times after it had undergone Persian rule:

> Nothing was in its former place,
> the South being in turmoil,
> the North in revolt.
> PETOSIRIS (Lichtheim 1980)

Political events, combined with the subsequent decline of tourism, clearly took its toll on the aspiring project. And yet, it was the *hope* that this land imparts that enabled me to continue: the hope that makes one work for something not because it stands a chance to succeed or will turn out well in the end, but because one believes it to be *good*. It seems that Petosiris was right when he said of Thoth:

> You have made my heart walk upon your waters,
> and who walks on your road will never stumble.
> PETOSIRIS (Jacq 1999)

New Hermopolis:
Description, composition, mission

New Hermopolis is an integrated model of development that consists of: (1) a *Green Farm*; (2) a *Hospitality Centre* (Eco-Retreat); and (3) a *Cultural Space* for the benefit of both the local community as well as the national and the international visitor. It lies between village and desert landscapes at the very heart of the antiquities of this region.

The Green Farm at New Hermopolis extends over ten acres of cultivated olive groves. Its objective is to provide an example of farming that is desert friendly and possibly wealth creating. Despite their rarity here now, there is enough evidence to suggest that olive trees were indigenous in Egypt in ancient times. In fact, one of the most beautiful pieces of Egyptian art depicts an olive branch held by Akhenaten. Now kept in the Berlin Museum, this artefact was in fact found in Tuna El-Gebel, and provides the image we use for our brand of olive oil.

In addition to our olive trees, we also have a vineyard, palm trees, and a grove dedicated to the sacred sycamore tree that, despite the significance of its symbolism, is currently threatened by extinction. This grove has now been made into a commemorative path of sycamores named after those who supported this project one way or another, in addition to those who influenced me throughout my life and contributed to my making.

FIGURE 14.

The Lady of the Sycamore.
The goddess Hathor appears to Sennedjem and his wife.
Tomb of Sennedjem, Deir el-Medina (Theban Necropolis).
Nineteenth Dynasty.

FIGURE 15.

Fragment of a temple relief depicting Akhenat-en with an olive branch; Amarna, Eighteenth Dynasty (Photograph: Richard Mortel; Ägyptisches Museum & Papyrussammlung, Berlin).

The Hospitality Centre (Eco-Retreat) is built at the centre of the land against a back drop of mountain scenery and maintains a free, open flow with our farm and the surrounding desert landscape. It is approached from the main gate through a long avenue lined with palm trees.

The retreat is built as a multi-domed stone structure, borrowing its distinctive, pointed-dome style from the local old buildings in the region, particularly the tombs of Tuna El-Gebel, El-Bersha, and Zawet Sultan. The emphasis on heritage extends to the building's doorways—every door is reclaimed and came with its own Egyptian history.

The design of the building follows ecological principles. Insulation and ventilation are maximised by the stone architecture and the layout of doors and windows as well as the shape of domes and vaults. Other aspects of environmental sustainability are maintained by using solar energy and the conscious consumption of water, which is drawn from our own private well. There is a rubbish-recycling area, and all the light fittings in the rooms are made from recycled iron by young Egyptian artists. As for the interiors, I was keen from the start to use natural fabric in all the furnishings, including Egyptian cotton.

The retreat itself consists of sixteen individual studios with a capacity for forty visitors. All are named after some of the writers, thinkers, and artists connected with the intellectual heritage of Hermopolis, as discussed in the previous chapters. The retreat as a whole is served by a large multi-functional reception room, dining room, swimming pool, and several outdoor seating areas.

The studios surround a square-shaped lotus pond, which should be regarded as a revival project in its own right. With this pond, we were successful in cultivating the Egyptian blue lotus (*Nymphæa cærulea*), which had long been considered extinct. It should also be noted that the studios—the rounded circle of each dome's base—combined with the square shape of the pond, form an octagon, representing both the geometric image of the unity of heaven and earth, and the eight divinities of the Hermopolitan creation myth.

The Cultural Space, on the other hand, has a library, which forms the first of three planned libraries aimed at different types of visitors. The existing library is a general-purpose collection geared towards the local population, and most of the books in this library are in Arabic. The projected libraries will include a general-purpose library for the international visitor, consisting of books in foreign languages, and a highly specialised collection for researchers dealing with the subject of Hermopolis, its ancient history, and its philosophy.

The Cultural Space also has a seminar and conference facility in addition to several indoor and outdoor exhibition and performance areas. Various avenues are now available for local youth to showcase their work to our visitors and their communities. In addition, the cultural space offers the opportunity to host lectures, training courses, intercultural events, as well as art exhibitions and musical performances. It is an open environment for local cultural groups, tourists, artists, writers, and other retreat groups.

Figure 16.

Blue Nymphæa Lotus (Nymphæa Cærulea).
Tomb of Nakht, Theban Necropolis, Luxor
Eighteenth Dynasty.

The New Hermopolis has been created to fulfil the following three goals:

1. To promote the concept of *heritage for development*, and to increase Egypt's awareness of its heritage as an important and largely untapped resource for development.
2. To introduce the concept of *intellectual tourism* based on the *intangible human heritage of ideas* that emanated from this region.
3. To create a *space for multiple belongings* inspired by the philosophy of ancient Hermopolis that managed to transcend the boundaries of its birthplace to include all the minds inspired by it, and whose creativity informed and developed its tradition.

Heritage for development

CULTURAL HERITAGE AND CULTURAL TOURISM

Culture and heritage are concepts that are commonly used today to refer to the legacies of the past. *Cultural heritage*, on the other hand, is the specific term used by UNESCO (2003) to declare World Heritage Sites in different parts of the world. Cultural heritage is typically divided into *tangible*, *natural*, and *intangible* forms.

Throughout this book, Hermopolis was discussed as an example of a heritage city with both *tangible* and *intangible* elements, both of which revealed themselves from the very beginning as the place where harmony was born (Nasser 2011). This is precisely the ethos that underpins any strategy for sustainable development which aims to promote harmony among human beings and between humanity and nature (WCED 1988).

The theme of cultural heritage and sustainable development began to emerge in the 1990s. By 2001, UNESCO regarded this form of heritage as the 'fourth pillar' of any sustainable development (Nurse 2006; Dallaire & Colbert 2012). This includes all forms of economic investment in cultural heritage, with tourism at the top of the list.

Notwithstanding the decline in tourist activity in Egypt in recent years, Egypt has in fact never fully benefited from its rich cultural heritage. Egypt's tourism—for decades— has long been governed by policies of *mass tourism*, which are dominated by controlled tourist experiences that often entail staying at large concrete hotels and resorts and moving between only a few select archæological sites. This strategy has primarily proven profitable to a handful of businessmen and big investors, while small businesses, social entrepreneurs, and local populations most often neither benefit from nor participate in the profits.

New Hermopolis, on the other hand, was set up as an innovative model of development combining eco-tourism, desert agriculture, and rural education in arts, culture, and heritage. All are embraced within the conceptual framework of *responsible and sustainable tourism*.

FIGURE 17.
The studios of New Hermopolis

At the core of the New Hermopolis initiative is the belief in *participatory tourism*, where the grassroots population are active players in the process. Through our heritage awareness and education programme, we highlight to the locals the heritage wealth of this region, and instil in them a sense of pride and ownership of this heritage. Besides the normal guided trips to antiquities sites, we encourage increased connection and engagement with the local community and its culture. This includes sharing in co-creative activities such as traditional music, farming practices, the training of artisans, and Egyptian cooking classes that aim to link gastronomy to the local cultural landscape. In addition, through our *Art Residency Programme*, we also welcome international artists, writers, musicians—anyone interested in cross-cultural sharing—for longer periods of stay. Mixing and exchanges between locals and foreigners is encouraged to redefine perceptions, challenge negative stereotypes, and widen the scope of participation and collaboration. The overall aim is to ensure that our visitors leave with a better appreciation for local communities and a sense of having participated in a worthwhile and socially responsible project.

The New Hermopolis retreat centre is the primary driver of revenue and has recently suffered due to the region's political turmoil and the decline in tourism. This in fact opened our eyes to the volatile nature of tourism, and the necessity to pay more attention to other forms of economic investment in heritage, even if, in many instances, the ultimate success of such activities is still dependant on tourism.

OTHER FORMS OF HERITAGE-INSPIRED ECONOMY

1. Farming and Hospitality Industries

New Hermopolis is currently working closely with local farmers to increase their awareness of sustainable desert agricultural practices and organic farming methods. Several collaborative programmes are underway, including the creation of marketable food products, production of olive oil, compost making, and wood manufacturing from palm tree refuse.

It is important to mention that the food we serve at New Hermopolis is by and large inspired by Egypt's traditional cuisine. It is prepared and served by well-selected and well-trained female villagers. This is part of an on-going outreach programme with the local village of Tuna El-Gebel to revive Egypt's rural cuisine and offer local women skills in catering and hospitality. We are now expanding this to create satellite catering and hospitality homes in the local village. In the future, these would work autonomously and would create their own small, independent businesses.

Our outreach programme is also extended to include the Youth Centre at Tuna El-Gebel, where we offer training in employment skills as well as capacity building, with a view of enhancing the chances for the local youth to seek employment either within the remit of the New Hermopolis initiative, or in the open market. As a matter of fact, our entire workforce, including housekeeping, maintenance, farming, gardening, and security are all drawn from the local villages we serve.

2.   Art and Creative Industries

In addition to general employment training, New Hermopolis is also offering the local youth a cultural programme that
aims to encourage and cultivate local talents. This includes introduction and training in various art forms, as well as making
our space available for showcasing these artistic talents. Time
and again, expression through the arts has been demonstrated
as an effective tool for building tolerant, open-minded, and
respectful societies. Art is known to promote critical thinking and to shed light upon issues that are difficult to address
head-on, encouraging constructive dialogue and social cohesion. Art in its wider sense is perhaps the only way to achieve
community harmony and to build a stronger sense of ownership of the local heritage.

Our *Art Programme* is also done with an eye on creative
industries, which are normally defined as industries that have
their origin in an individual's creativity, skill, or talent, and
which have the potential for wealth and job creation through
using one's intellectual capital. This definition encompasses
architecture, craft, design, film-making, music, as well as the
performing arts. However, in this initiative we do not rely sole-
ly on the intellectual capital of the individual, but also on the
intellectual capital of the place itself, as reflected in its unique
heritage and its distinctive traditions. Therefore, the provided
training includes creative writing, journalism, acting, videog-
raphy, and more; its ethos is rooted in engaging local heritage
and ethnic art to generate new ideas and experiences.

The funding for all the training workshops comes either

from the retreat revenue or through small donations. Some are offered free of charge by volunteer artists, and the rest is still funded by myself.

With the emphasis on investment in people, our scheme should be able to establish, in the long run, a network of cultural entrepreneurs who will in turn have the chance to create new work opportunities in the art market for themselves. As part of this scheme, we specifically attempt to address the needs of the local mass of educated unemployed youth who are unable to find themselves in a traditional job market. Through this, we hope to contribute towards the emergence of a heritage-focused economic community that is also fully aware of the need to protect and preserve their past.

Intellectual tourism: Itineraries of the mind

The concept of *intellectual tourism* is a new approach that considers human thought and the progression of ideas through time and space as a form of *intangible heritage*. This notion is yet to receive the attention it deserves, which is why it is dealt with separately from other forms of cultural tourism.

In intellectual tourism, *itineraries of the mind* are devised through linking the visitor to centres in the world that evolved over time as spaces of knowledge, namely: places endowed with intellectual capital, or in other words: centres credited with the ability for specific thought generation and production (Nasser 2011; 2012; 2018). However, these centres cannot be conceived or understood except through their material presence in time and space, and that understanding cannot rest at a literal level, free of imagination.

Throughout this book, the emphasis has not been placed on the physical attributes of Hermopolis as a 'monument', but on the *body of thought* that this site inspired. The tourists who normally visit the tangible site and its surrounding antiquities are also encouraged to look beyond the physical monument and its historicity to find hidden meanings and to create new narratives. This is why we at New Hermopolis were keen to revive the ancient Egyptian Festival of Thoth. This festival used to take place in ancient times in the month of Thoth (or Tot) as an homage to the *creative word*, the very essence of the Hermopolitan philosophy.

The first Thoth festival that took place at New Hermopolis was held in October 2015, and has been repeated annually at the same time of year. This festival is not meant to revive ancient rituals, but to demonstrate how the ancients respected the *creative word* and the *innate creativity of the human mind*. The proceedings of the festival usually include poetry readings, interactive theatre, improvisation, storytelling, art exhibitions, as well as musical and dance performances. Our festival of Thoth is still at an early stage, and is only presently conducted on a local level. We do hope, however, that one day that Thoth's Festival will grow and find its way into the international cultural events calendar. The model we have in mind for this is the Hay on Wye Festival in the United Kingdom, which transformed an ordinary village in rural Wales into an international capital of books and literary achievements.

FIGURE 18.

Poster for the second Thoth's Festival
New Hermopolis, 2016.

There are now Hay Festivals in Bangladesh, Colombia, Kenya, Ireland, Lebanon, Mexico, and Spain, and it seems that it is now the right time to have a Hay Festival in the city of Thoth, who conveyed all art and knowledge to humanity.

Usually, the main purpose of such festivals is to bring together creative minds from different backgrounds and walks of life in order to think about the world in different ways; to formulate creative and imaginative solutions to some of the most urgent problems we face. The celebration of Thoth/Hermes in this festival is a further declaration and affirmation of the literary and creative nature of his terrain. This is likely to be a major attraction for the cultural tourist who would also be interested in the intellectual itineraries we offer.

In devising these itineraries, we make an imaginative use of the geo-Hermetica belt discussed in chapter one. This concept was initially proposed to connect the city of Hermes—Hermopolis—with the city of alchemy—Panopolis—as well as to the seat of the famous Gnostic library at Nag Hammadi in Egypt. Other geo-Hermetic routes could also include Lycopolis, where the philosopher Plotinus was born, and the great cosmopolis of Alexandria, where the *Hermetica* was discovered, and where all the intellectual endeavours of that time evolved. The notion of the Hermetica belt also has the potential of going beyond the territorial specificity of this heritage to include all the minds that were inspired and influenced by Hermopolitan philosophy: all those whose creativity informed and developed this continuing tradition and contributed to its ongoing regeneration and reproduction.

Perhaps what we need to do is develop something like a

'world memory map' that sees the figures associated with the Hermetic tradition as carriers and transmitters of this heritage, while the cities they come from can become landmarks on these Hermetic routes. This approach could go a long way to safeguarding the intellectual capital of Hermeticism from succumbing to stagnation and segregation. Above all, Hermetic intellectual tourism targets a niche market of people who are seeking pilgrimage not only to destinations in the outer world, but also to those in the inner world through self-transformation and the expansion of consciousness.

A designed space for multiple belonging

Many people ask me why I gave up on my life-long profession as a psychiatrist to embark upon a project that many see as a deviation from where I belong. Ironically however, the issue of 'belonging' has always been my prime concern; in fact it has been at the forefront of all my psychiatric research into the interface between mind, culture, and identity.

There is no doubt that in our contemporary world we all live with an internal clamour of identities: gender, race, nationality, class, political affiliation, and so forth. These are the components of our personality that have been referred to as the 'genes of the soul', even if most of them are far from being innate (Brain Pickings 2015).

Based on his own experience of those clamouring identities, the Lebanese-French writer Maalouf (2012) emphasised the need to embrace the notion of 'multiple belongings' in

order to avoid the exclusion and 'otherness' that, in his opinion, is responsible for the violence we see in our world today.
Denying a legitimate aspect of a person's identity and defining them through a given set of criteria is bound to lead, as I
predicted years ago, to the phenomenon of the 'misfit' and to
'subcultures of extremism' (Nasser 1997). Fortunately, not all
who find themselves in this predicament go down this path.
Some decide instead to develop themselves, claiming all they
see as rightly theirs, and in the process, they truly grow.

This is very much my own personal experience. I was born
in Egypt and raised with Arabic as my mother tongue; and yet
I lived and worked in England for many years, where I was
seen and judged through the myopic eye of race and gender.
Looking back on this, I suppose what helped me most was another dimension to my soul, namely the Egyptian history that
I felt comfortable inhabiting.

Hermopolis was for me the ultimate destination for those
who seek to truly belong to a world where barriers and fron-
tiers no longer exist. The revival of this ancient city is not
meant to venerate a specific history but rather to bring back
the spirit of a place that once had the capacity to embrace and
hold all.

New Hermopolis clearly has elements in common with
the concept of 'intentional' or 'utopian' communities, particularly in its orientation towards ecological lifestyles. It is none-
theless very different from the idea of the 'commune' (Christian 2003). It is not about groups deciding to live together
based on shared ideas or beliefs. It welcomes all who believe
in the wider definition of *ecological citizenship*, and who hope

that their efforts will impact not only on earth, but those who live upon it.

Despite its romantic symbolism, this project is not a search for a lost paradise. It does not seek to create an ideal city, but rather a *city of ideas* that can demonstrate how the knowledge of the past can benefit the present and contribute towards the building of a more tolerant and sustainable future.

New Hermopolis is certainly an ambitious project that will never be able to deliver its true mission to the world and achieve its full potential as a model of enlightenment and development for Egypt without proper recognition, support, and funding. And yet, what it needs most is to transcend the person who created it, and to become part of a much larger framework.

The idea of reviving ancient Hermopolis is perhaps not unlike the recent revival of the ancient library of Alexandria. Therefore, I intend to donate New Hermopolis upon my death to the State of Egypt, and intend for it to become part of the great Bibliotheca Alexandrina. In doing this, it is my hope that the time will come for Alexandria to connect once again to the city of its early beginnings.

> Oh, Sycamore of Hermopolis
> which gives me air from within itself
> I embrace the place at Hermopolis
> If it flourishes, I flourish
> If it lives I live.
> THE BOOK OF THE DEAD § 59

CHRISTIAN, A. 2003. *Creating a Life Together: Practical Tools to Grow Ecovillages and Intentional Communities.* Gabriola Island: New Society Publishers.

COLBERT, F. 2012. 'Financing the Arts: Some Issues for a Mature Market'. *Megatrend Review: The International Review of Applied Economics* 9.1: 83–96.

COPENHAVER, B.P. 1992. *Hermetica: The Greek Corpus Hermeticum and the Latin Asclepius in a New English Translation, with Notes and Introduction.* Cambridge: Cambridge University Press.

CRONIN, V. 1967. *The Florentine Renaissance.* London: Collins.

DALLIER, G., & F. COLBERT. 2012. 'Sustainable Development and Cultural Policy: Do They Make a Happy Marriage?' *ENCATC: Journal of Cultural Management and Policy* 2.1: 6–11.

DAWKINS, P. 1984. *Dedication to the Light.* Northampton: Francis Bacon Research Trust.

DZIELSKA, M. 2002. *Hypatia of Alexandria.* Translated by F. Lyra. Cambridge, MA: Harvard University Press.

EBELING, F. 2007. *The Secret History of Hermes Trismegistus: Hermeticism from Ancient to Modern Times.* Translated by David Lorton. Ithaca, NY: Cornell University Press.

ECO, U. 1990. *The Limits of Interpretation.* Bloomington, IN: Indiana University Press.

EL-DALY, O. 2005. *Egyptology: The Missing Millennium. Ancient Egypt in Medieval Arabic Writing.* London: UCL Press.

EMERSON, R. W., & J. NEEDLEMAN. 2008. *The Spiritual Emerson.* New York: Penguin Group.

FAIVRE, A. 2000. *Theosophy, Imagination, Tradition: Studies in Western Esotericism.* Translated by Christine Rhone. SUNY Series in Western Esoteric Traditions. Albany, NY: State University of New York Press.

FAULKNER, R. O. 2007. *The Ancient Egyptian Coffin Texts.* Oxford: Aris & Philips.

———., & O. GOELET. 2008. *The Egyptian Book of the Dead.* San Francisco: Chronicle Books.

FOSTER, J., & S. T. HOLLIS, eds. 1996. *Hymns, Prayers, and Songs: An Anthology of Ancient Egyptian Lyric Poetry.* Writings from the Ancient World 8. Atlanta, GA: Scholars Press.

FOWDEN, G. 1986. *The Egyptian Hermes: A Historical Approach to the Late Pagan Mind.* Princeton, NJ: Princeton University Press.

FRANKL, V. 2006. *Man's Search for Meaning.* Boston, MA: Beacon Press.

FREKE, T., & P. GANDY. 1999. *The Hermetica: The Lost Wisdom of the Pharaohs.* New York: Tarcher/Penguin.

FRENCH, P. J. 1972. *John Dee: The World of an Elizabethan Magus.* London: Routledge.

GEBSER, J. 1986. *The Ever-Present Origin.* Translated by Noel Barstad and Algis Mickunas. Athens: Ohio University Press.

GODWIN, J., C. CHANEL, & J. P. DEVENEY. 1995. *The Hermetic Brotherhood of Luxor: Initiatic and Historical Documents of an*

Order of Practical Occultism. York Beach, ME: Samuel Weiser.

GRIFFITH, F. L. 1926. 'The Teaching of Amenophis the Son of Kanakht. Papyrus B.M. 10474'. *Journal of Egyptian Archæology* 12.3–4: 191–231.

HAMBLIN, W. J., & D. R. SEELY. 2007. *Solomon's Temple: Myth and History.* London: Thames & Hudson.

HANSEN, M. H. 2006. *Polis: An Introduction to the Ancient Greek City State.* Oxford. Oxford University Press.

HERMANS, H. J. M. 2001. 'The Dialogical Self: Toward a Theory of Personal and Cultural Positioning'. *Culture & Psychology* 7: 243–281.

HORNUNG, E. 1992. *Idea into Image: Essays on Ancient Egyptian Thought.* Translated by E. Berdeck. New York: Timken.

_____. 2001. *The Secret Lore of Egypt: Its Impact on the West.* Translated by David Lorton. Ithaca, NY: Cornell University Press.

_____. 2001. *Akhenaten and the Religion of Light.* Translated by David Lorton. Ithaca, NY: Cornell University Press.

IBN ARABI SOCIETY. 2013. 'Ibn Arabi and Rumi, Being Fully Human'. Conference organised by Ibn Arabi Society and the Graduate Theological Union in Berkley, May 3–4, 2013.

JACKSON, L. 2011. *Thoth: The History of the Ancient Egyptian God of Wisdom.* Glastonbury: Avalonia.

JACQ, C. 1999. *The Living Wisdom of Ancient Egypt.* London: Simon & Schuster.

JAMES, W. 1950. *The Principles of Psychology.* 2 volumes. Revised Edition. New York: Dover Publications.

_____. 2008. *The Varieties of Religious Experience: A Study in Human Nature: Being the Gifford Lectures on Natural Religion delivered at Edinburgh in 1901–1902*. New York: Routledge.

_____. 2017. *A Pluralistic Universe*. NP: Alpha Editions.

JASNOW, R., & K. ZAUZICH. 2005. *The Ancient Egyptian Book of Thoth*. Wiesbaden: Harrassowwitz.

JUNG, C. G. 1957. *The Psychology of the Unconscious*. Translated by R. F. C. Hull. New York: Dodd, Mead.

_____. 1968. *Psychology and Alchemy*. Translated by R. F. C. Hull. London: Routledge.

_____. 2006. *The Undiscovered Self*. Translated by R. F. C. Hull. New York: Signet.

KASTER, J. 1993. *The Wisdom of Ancient Egypt: Writings from the Time of the Pharaohs*. New York: Barnes & Noble.

KEMP, B. 2011. 'Akhenaton's City and the Lure of Inconsistency'. In *Proceedings of the Conference, Alexandria and Other Centres of Thought in Ancient Egypt, 10–11 December 2009*. Edited by Mervat Nasser & Sahar Hammouda. Alexandria: Bibliotheca Alexandrina.

KREIS, S. 2000. 'From Polis to Cosmopolis: Alexander the Great and the Hellenistic World, 323-30 BC'. *Lectures on Ancient and Medieval European History* 9. Revised 05 February 2010. http://historyguide.org/

LACHMAN, G. 2007. *Rudolf Steiner: An Introduction to his Life and Work*. New York: Tarcher.

_____. 2011. *The Quest for Hermes Trismegistus: From Ancient*

Egypt to the Modern Word. Edinburgh: Floris Books.

———. 2015. *The Secret Teachers of the Western World*. New York: Tarcher.

LICHTHEIM, M. 1973. *Ancient Egyptian Literature, Volume I: The Old and Middle Kingdoms*. Berkeley: University of California Press.

———. 1976. *Ancient Egyptian Literature, Volume II: The New Kingdom*. Berkeley: University of California Press.

———. 1980. *Ancient Egyptian Literature, Volume III: The Late Period*. Berkeley: University of California Press.

LINDSAY, J. 1970. *The Origins of Alchemy in Græco-Roman Egypt*. London: Frederick Muller.

MAALOUF, A. 2012. *In the Name of Identity: Violence and the Need to Belong*. Translated by Barbara Bray. New York: Arcade Publishing.

MACY, J., & C. JOHNSTON. 2012. *Active Hope: How to Face the Mess we're in Without going Crazy*. Novato, CA: New World Library.

MAY, R. 1999. *Freedom and Destiny*. New York: W. W. Norton.

NASSER, M. 1997. *Culture and Weight Consciousness*. London: Routledge.

———. 2004. *Why Did Horus Lose his Eye? A New Reading in Ancient Egyptian Thought* (Arabic). Cairo: El Shaquia Publications.

———. 2011. 'The Enduring Legacy of Ancient Hermopolis in

Western Thought'. In *Alexandria and Other Centres of Thought in Ancient Egypt, 10–11 December 2009* (Conference Proceedings). Edited by M. Nasser & S. Hammouda. Alexandria: Bibliotheca Alexandrina.

_____. 2012. 'New Hermopolis—Revival of an Ancient Capital of Thought: A Project for our Time'. In *Capital Cities and Heritage in the Globalisation Era*. Conference Proceedings. Edited by H. Saidi & S. Sagnes. Quebec: Laval University.

_____. 2018. 'Hermopolis: Intellectual Tourism and Itineraries of the Mind'. In *Heritage 2018: Proceedings of the 6th International Conference on Heritage and Sustainable Development, 12–15 June 2018*. Edited by R. Amoeda, S. Lira, J. M. Santiago Zaragoza, J. Calvo Serrano, & F. Garcia Carillo. Granada.

NÉRET, G., NAPOLEON, EMPEROR OF THE FRENCH, & COMMISSION DES SCIENCES ET ARTS D'ÉGYPTE. 2002. *Description de l'Égypte*. Köln: Taschen.

NOVALIS. 2005. *The Novices at Sais*. New York: Archipelago.

OCKINGA, B. 1986. 'Amenophis, Son of Hapu—A Biographical Sketch'. *The Rundle Foundation for Egyptian Archaeology* 18: 3–6.

PETZET, M. 2009. 'Genus Loci: The Spirit of Monuments and Sites'. In *Spirit of Place: Between Tangible and Intangible Heritage*. Edited by L. Turgeon. Québec: Les Presses de l'Université Laval.

PAOVA, M. 2015. 'The Genes of the Soul: Amin Maalouf on Belonging, Conflict, and How we Inhabit our Identity'. www.brainpickings.org

PARACELSUS. 1967. *The Hermetic and Alchemical Writings of Aureolus Phillippus Theophrastus Bombast of Hohenheim, Called Paracelsus, the Great: Now for the First Time Faithfully and Accurately Translated into English.* Edited and translated by A. E. Waite. New York: University Books.

PETERS, F. E. 1990. 'Hermes and Harran'. In *Intellectual Studies on Islam: Essays Written in Honour of Martin B. Dickson.* Edited by M. Mazzaoui and V. B. Moreen. Salt Lake City: University of Utah.

PLIMER, R. A. 2014. *An Introduction to Hermetic Philosophy.* 3 volumes. Bembridge: Courtyard Publications.

POLLARD, J., & H. REID. 2006. *The Rise and Fall of Alexandria.* New York: Viking.

QUIRKE, S. 2011. 'On/Heliopolis/Ain Shams: Where Light First Became Enlightenment'. In *Alexandria and Other Centres of Thought in Ancient Egypt: Proceedigs of the Conference, 10–11 December 2009.* Edited by M. Nasser & S. Hammouda. Alexandria: Bibliotheca Alexandrina

RICE, M. 1997. *Egypt's Legacy: The Archetypes of Western Civilisation: 3000–30 BC.* London: Routledge.

RILKE, R. M. 1939. *Duino Elegies.* Translated by J. B Leishman & S. Spenser. New York: Norton.

ROBINSON, J., R. SMITH, & THE COPTIC GNOSTIC LIBRARY PROJECT. 1988. *The Nag Hammadi Library in English.* San Francisco: Harper & Row.

SACKS, S. 2011. 'Social Sculpture and New Organs of Perception: New Practices and New Pedagogy for a Humane & Ecologically

Viable Future'. In *Beuysian Legacies in Ireland and Beyond: Art, Culture, and Politics*. Edited by C.-M. Lerm-Hayes. Berlin: LIT.

SOLNIT, R. 2016. *Hope in the Dark: Untold History, Wild Possibilities*. Chicago, IL: Haymarket Books.

SHEPHERD, K. R. D. 2010. 'The Egyptian Sufi Dhu-l-Nun Al-Misri'. www.citizenthought.net

SHEPHERD, M. 1999. *Friend to Mankind: Marsilio Ficino (1433–1499)*. London: Shepheard-Walwyn.

SLAVENBURG, J. 2012. *The Hermetic Link: From Secret Tradition to Modern Thought*. Lake Worth, FL: Ibis Press.

TWINCH, C. 2010. 'Created for Compassion. Ibn 'Arabī's Work on Dhū-l-Nūn the Egyptian'. *Journal of the Muhyiddin Ibn 'Arabi Society* 47.

UNESCO. 2001. 'High-Level Round Table on Cultural Diversity and Biodiversity for Sustainable Development'. Jointly organised by UNEP in Johannesburg (South Africa) during the World Summit on Sustainable Development, 3 Sept 2002.

_____. 2003. 'Defining World Heritage'. www.unesco.org

WASSERMAN, J. 2005. *The Mystery Traditions: Secret Symbols and Sacred Art*. Rochester, VT: Destiny Books.

WILSON, P. L. 2007. 'The Disciples at Sais: A Sacred Theory of Earth'. In *Green Hermeticism: Alchemy and Ecology*. Edited by P. Lamborn Wilson, C. Bamford, and K. Townley. Great Barrington, MA: Lindisfarne Books.

_____. 2007. 'Green Hermiticism'. In *Green Hermeticism: Alchemy and Ecology*. Edited by P. Lamborn Wilson, C. Bamford, and

K. Townley. Great Barrington, MA: Lindisfarne Books.

WILSON, P. L., C. BAMFORD, & K. TOWNLEY, eds. 2007. *Green Hermeticism: Alchemy and Ecology.* Great Barrington, MA: Lindisfarne Books.

WORLD COMMISSION ON CULTURE & DEVELOPMENT. 1988. UNESCO publishing House.

YATES, F. A. 1991. *Giordano Bruno and the Hermetic Tradition.* Chicago: University of Chicago Press.

_____. 1972. *The Rosicrucian Enlightenment.* London: Routledge & Kegan Paul.

YEATS, W. B. 1933. *The Winding Stair and Other Poems.* London: Macmillan & Co.

ABOUT THE AUTHOR

DR. MERVAT ABDEL NASSER (MD, MPHIL, FRCPSYCH) is a consultant psychiatrist, researcher in Egyptology, and writer. Graduate of Cairo Medical School and fellow of the Royal College of Psychiatrists, Dr. Nasser holds a masters in philosophy and a doctorate in psychiatry from London University. She also has two diplomas in moral philosophy and the history of medicine.

Having served as an academic and psychiatrist in England from 1977–2007, her clinical practice focused on general adult psychiatry with a special interest in the field of culture and mental health. She has a special interest in theories of education and integrative models of teaching, which are reflected in her her work as a writer, academic, and clinical tutor. She has written psychological and philosophical commentaries on ancient Egyptian thought, collected in her book *Why did Horus Lose his Eye: A New Reading of Ancient Egyptian Thought*. She has also written several books in Arabic addressed to the young reader, including an award-winning illustrated children's series.

In 2007, Mervat took early retirement from her job as consultant psychiatrist and senior lecturer at King's College and returned to Egypt to pursue her dream of establishing the New Hermopolis. She has since dedicated herself entirely to this cause.

CPSIA information can be obtained
at www.ICGtesting.com
Printed in the USA
BVHW071041150621
609528BV00004B/989